BOYS FROM THE

Boys From the Blackstuff

Five plays for television by

ALAN BLEASDALE

GRANADA
London Toronto Sydney New York

Published by Granada Publishing Limited in 1983

ISBN 0 586 05980 6

A Granada Paperback Original
Copyright © Alan Bleasdale 1982, 1983

Acknowledgements are due to
J. M Dent & Sons Ltd for the use of a
quotation from *Do Not Go Gentle Into
That Good Night* by Dylan Thomas

Granada Publishing Limited
Frogmore, St Albans, Herts AL2 2NF
and
36 Golden Square, London W1R 4AH
515 Madison Avenue, New York, NY 10022, USA
117 York Street, Sydney, NSW 2000, Australia
60 International Blvd, Rexdale, Ontario, R9W 6J2, Canada
61 Beach Road, Auckland, New Zealand

Printed and bound in Great Britain by
Hazell Watson & Viney Ltd, Aylesbury
Set in Baskerville

Granada ®
Granada Publishing ®

Boys From the Blackstuff

Jobs for the Boys

CHRISSIE TODD   Michael Angelis
LOGGO LOGMOND   Alan Igbon
YOSSER HUGHES   Bernard Hill
GEORGE MALONE   Peter Kerrigan
DIXIE DEAN   Tom Georgeson
KEVIN DEAN   Gary Bleasdale

At the DOE
DONALD MOSS   David Ross
LAWTON   David Neilson
CHRISSIE'S CLERK   Monica Brown
LOGGO'S CLERK   Simon Meryl
DIXIE'S CLERK   Gilly Coman
YOSSER'S CLERK   John Dee

GEORGE'S CLERK   Isa Dixon

At the Building Site
SNOWY MALONE   Chris Darwin
MALLOY   Shay Gorman
JIMMY JOHNSON   Vince Earl
POLICEMAN   Clive Russell
ARTHUR   Bill Moores
COUNCIL WORKER   Ron Metcalfe

Yosser's Children
JASON   Timothy Bleasdale
ANNE MARIE   Tamana Bleasdale
DUSTIN   Jamie Bleasdale

1.   Exterior. Department of Employment Building. Day.

We establish the Department building. A series of shots: two workmen; a girl in white talking to a man; a man with bucket; the girl in white and the man; a Rastafarian. We see the DOE building. We hear the traffic going past.

2.   Interior. Department of Employment Building. Day.

We see the interior of the DOE. Two general points of view show clerks at work. We see Chrissie, and we are aware of the counter clerk who is behind a wire mesh grille. We see Chrissie and the others in turn through this grille. Like caged animals.

CLERK. Name.

CHRISSIE. (*Misses a beat.*) Christopher Todd.

CLERK. Full name. (*Takes out a file.*)

CHRISSIE. (*Quietly.*) Christopher Robin Todd. (*Shrugs.*) It was me Mam. (*Turns head.*)

Freeze.

We see Loggo. He is looking at his gold watch, and is expensively and well dressed.

LOGGO. Wha'? Course I want a job. I'm desperate. But look, no offence meant like, but we've been through all this before an' well, y' have already made me miss me golf lessons.

CLERK. Look, these matters take time . . .

LOGGO. What I'm sayin' is, get a move on, will y', cos I'm supposed t'be at the Haydock races for half-past two. There's a good boy.

Freeze.

We see Yosser with his three children. He is leaning forward.

CLERK. The procedure of a test check is just a formality, Mr Hughes. However, I'm afraid—

YOSSER. Afraid? Y'll be terrified in a minute. (*Leans in.*) Now sort me soddin' Giro check out before I knock y' into the disability department.

Freeze.

We see George, who appears to be dressed in working clothes, but we can only see the top half of him.

CLERK. If you could just wait there, Mr Malone . . .

She goes to a filing cabinet.

GEORGE. Come on, girl. I should've been on site half an hour ago.

CLERK. (*Hesitant.*) Yeah. (*Opens filing cabinet.*)

GEORGE. (*Backing away.*) I don't like to let the boys down, you know. I mean, there'll be ten ton of the black stuff on the deck by now, waitin' for me.

We see the clerk, then George. He is wearing pyjama bottoms and slippers.

Freeze.

A row of men are waiting on a bench. Another row of men are waiting at the counter. We see Dixie.

CLERK. Dependants Mr Dean?

DIXIE. Yeah, a wife and four kids. Two at school and two on the dole.

CLERK. Ah yes, but unfortunately the two on the dole don't count for—

DIXIE. No one on the dole counts, friend.

Freeze.

*Two men peer through a barely open door leading to the interior offices of the Department. The door has a sign –
'UNEMPLOYMENT OFFICE' – which is the euphemism for the fraud section. Both men are in their thirties and are wearing stock fashionless office suits. The younger of the two who will emerge as*

the driver (Lawton) mutters to the other one, his passenger (Moss). They come out.

LAWTON. (*Driver.*) Hey, there's one of them. Todd.

We see Lawton's point of view of Chrissie. He focuses on Chrissie. Moss joins him at the door, then walks off. We come back to Chrissie.

CLERK. It seems from your files, Mr Todd, that one of our inspectors has visited your house on two separate occasions during the past ten days without receiving any answer.

We see Moss watching Chrissie.

CHRISSIE. Ah what a shame.

CLERK. You were out?

CHRISSIE. Looks that way, doesn't it?

CLERK. Can you tell me where you were?

CHRISSIE. I might be able to if you tell me when you called.

CLERK. It's the . . . morning of Tuesday the third, and . . . the afternoon of Thursday the twelfth.

There is a pause.

CHRISSIE. Haven't a clue.

CLERK. Were you employed during those two days?

CHRISSIE. Who me?

CLERK. Look, have you got a job, Mr Todd?

CHRISSIE. Oh yeah, I just come here f'the company and the pleasant surroundings.

CLERK. (*Patiently, and not without sympathy.*) You haven't anwered the question.

CHRISSIE. (*Looking away.*) I haven't worked in over a year.

CLERK. Right, Mr Todd, that's all.

Chrissie stands.

We will, however, be making further visits to your house in due course.

CHRISSIE. I'll bake a cake.

Chrissie walks away. We hear the clerk call the next contestant.

CLERK. Next.

We see the DOE hall at work. Chrissie walks towards the entrance.

3. Interior. Entrance hall of DOE Building. Day.

A man, Arthur, is waiting. Chrissie comes from the hall into the doorway of the building, and sees Arthur with his back turned, facing a window ledge. He is looking down at the racing section of The Daily Mirror, *marking off some horses with a pen. Chrissie approaches him, and stands beside him. He looks over his shoulder at the paper.*

CHRISSIE. Carnations are red in Albania this winter. Comrade. (*He winks at Arthur.*)

ARTHUR. Say that again Chrissie.

CHRISSIE. Ah, y'alright. You got anythin' for me? (*He puts his arm around Arthur's shoulder, and stares down at the paper.*)

ARTHUR. Malloy's been askin' after you. (*Looks at Chrissie.*)

CHRISSIE. That's nice of him. Go on.

ARTHUR. Bricks and wheels.

Chrissie nods.

Fourteen notes.

CHRISSIE. You're on.

Chrissie nods again. Arthur looks behind him for a second, then gets an envelope out of his pocket as Chrissie looks behind himself as well.

ARTHUR. The van'll be at the end of your road in the mornin'. The keys'll be in the teapot on the dashboard.

Arthur gives Chrissie the envelope. Chrissie puts it in his inside pocket. They focus on the racing section. Chrissie points at the paper. He moves round.

CHRISSIE. Teacher's Pet in the 3.15.

ARTHUR. Ah, well, I don't follow the horses, Chrissie. I only look at this so that . . . *(He looks behind again.)*

CHRISSIE. I'd bet my life on it. In fact I'd go so far as to say it was an absolute certainty.

Arthur looks at him, then at the paper, then back at Chrissie.

ARTHUR. How do you know that?

CHRISSIE. It's yesterday's paper. *(He half turns, then turns back.)* Y'd never make a spy, Arthur.

Chrissie pushes Arthur and goes out. Arthur leaves too.

4.   Exterior. Wasteland. Before dawn.

Chrissie gets into a Transit van. He takes the keys and a note out of the teapot, and starts the van. He reads the instructions and drives off.

4a. Exterior. Traffic lights. Early morning. Just before dawn.

We see Chrissie in a 30-cwt Ford Transit van. He is on his own. Then we see a Morris Marina van behind the Transit. It swerves to follow the Transit. But this is not a big moment, it is not dwelt on.

5.   Exterior. A housing estate. Early morning. A few minutes later.

The sky is now a shade lighter. Chrissie is driving, slowly through a housing estate in the Transit van. He has the instructions in his hands as he drives.

6.   Exterior. Wasteland. Day.

Chrissie is driving across a patch of wasteland. Then he runs the van up on some waste ground towards the back gardens of a row of houses. As he gets out of the Transit the Marina van parks nearby. Again this is not a big moment. Shadowy. If it is noticed at all, we shouldn't be certain if it is the same van as in Scene 4a. We follow Chrissie as he starts across the wasteland. He goes past the remnants of an adventure playground with broken goalposts. There are three-legged chairs and mouldy mattresses lying on the ground.

7. Exterior. Jimmy Johnson's back garden. Day.

Chrissie gets to the back gardens, and counts them quickly from one end of the row. When he finds the right garden, he tests the fence, but it won't give way or come loose. It is shoulder-height and there is a hole in it. Chrissie looks at the house which is all in darkness. He starts to struggle underneath the fence feet first. We hear a door being opened and shut quietly. We see Jimmy Johnson scurrying down the garden. He climbs onto the fence further down the garden. Chrissie is halfway under and stuck.

CHRISSIE. Friggin' hell. *(He looks up.)*

JIMMY. Very good. Our dog can't get through there.

CHRISSIE. *(Laughing.)* Jimmy Johnson.

JIMMY. *(He nods.)* Correct.

Jimmy vaults over the fence.

JIMMY. Come 'head. We've only got three seconds before the searchlights hit us.

He moves away.

CHRISSIE. Hey, give us a hand will 'y.

Jimmy comes back, pulls Chrissie out of the hole. They run across to the Transit.

8. Exterior. Loggo's house. Day.

It is still early morning, but is later and lighter again. We see Loggo with a wickerware basket and three fishing rods. He is wearing waterproofs and a fisherman's hat with a couple of flights in the head band. He saunters to the corner of the road, quietly singing 'Old Man River' in a bass voice with Alabama intonations. He gets to the alleyway that runs parallel with the main road he has been walking towards. He turns into it, quickens his pace, and heads towards the end of the alleyway. Even though it is no more than twenty yards away, we cannot see what he is approaching. Then we see the Transit backed into the alleyway. Loggo opens the back doors, enters the Transit and sits down.

CHRISSIE. What's this with the fishing gear?

LOGGO. Picked it up in the Shetlands. Bugger all else t'do up there.

CHRISSIE. Ever caught anythin'?

LOGGO. Yeah. Course I did. First go.

CHRISSIE. What did y' catch?

LOGGO. Pneumonia.

Laughter. The Transit van moves off and turns right towards the main road. As it turns right we see the Marina start up and follow. The Transit turns into main road and the Marina goes in the same direction.

9. Exterior. George's road. Day.

We see a small 'estate' of old-fashioned terraced houses, surrounded by a bleak new estate, backing onto the River Mersey at Dingle. The area is riddled with blocked-off roads and sudden cul-de-sacs. The Transit van comes into George's road and goes down it for some distance. As it passes one of the houses we hear the horn beep once. The Transit continues for a while, then begins a three-point turn. Chrissie then takes the van back up the road. As he does so, the Marina van passes, going the other way. Chrissie stops his van, at the top of the road. As all this goes on, we hear Chrissie and Loggo inside the Transit.

LOGGO. This is George Malone's road, isn't it?

CHRISSIE. Yeah.

LOGGO. How is he?

CHRISSIE. He's in hospital. I went to see him last night.

LOGGO. How is he? I heard he's er y' know, sort of . . .

CHRISSIE. Yeah, he is.

LOGGO. Christ.

CHRISSIE. We're pickin' up one of his lads though, their Snowy.

LOGGO. Ah no, not him! Not Karl Marx lives.

CHRISSIE. He's alright, Loggo.

LOGGO. Oh aye, yeah. He's a barrel of laughs isn't he? I mean
I just love listenin' to the latest production figures for sugar
cane in Cuba. Especially when I'm havin' me dinner. I mean
I'm sometimes that fascinated I let me food go cold.

> *Snowy Malone comes out of the house. He is a plasterer and he*
> *appears to have been recently battered. He makes no attempt at hiding*
> *his trade, and has his working clothes on, flecked and stained with*
> *plaster. His haversack is over his shoulder and he is carrying a large*
> *coil of rope. He is physically small, but walks like John Conteh used*
> *to at the end of a good round. Snowy walks towards the top of the*
> *road and the Transit. He goes past the Marina van which is parked*
> *just by a lorry on the other side of the road, having not yet started its*
> *three-point turn. The Marina van appears to be empty. As Snowy*
> *approaches the back of the Transit, he looks up at the bedroom*
> *windows in one of the houses and sees a curtain move. He turns*
> *quickly and catches a glimpse of a woman at her window. He stops,*
> *looks up and shouts up.*

SNOWY. Yes, that's right. It's me again, love. Go ahead. Be
a solid citizen. Do the decent thing and report me. Don't keep
it a secret, whatever y' do.

> *The Transit comes backwards into vision as it reverses down the road.*
> *We see Loggo sitting inside.*

CHRISSIE. There's not much chance of that, Snowy. I mean,
after all, y've just told the whole soddin' street y'self.

LOGGO. Why don't y' buy a banner, bollocks? Or put an
announcement in the Echo. Get in.

Snowy crosses towards the Transit as he talks.

SNOWY. It's her – the minge bag. The dole'll give her a retirement party by the time she's sixty, they will.

She drops her curtain. Snowy reaches the back of the Transit and seems about to turn and shout at the woman's curtains again. Loggo practically lifts him up into the Transit. Chrissie drives off.

10.   Exterior. George's road/interior of the Marina. Day.

We see the Marina van, still apparently without driver or passenger. We hold on the Marina. Two men slowly come up into vision from the floor of the van. With no intention of it being comic. They are Moss and Lawton, previously seen at the dole office. They are now in working clothes, donkey jackets and jeans. They clamber into the front seats.

MOSS. *(Flatly.)* Well, that was good. I enjoyed that.

As the driver tries to start the van, the passenger pulls a cassette recorder out of his jacket pocket and speaks into it.

MOSS. Suspects have picked up . . . what's his name?

LAWTON. Malone.

Lawton is still hammering the ignition.

MOSS. *(Continuing to record.)* Malone in Freshfields Street and have turned left into Grafton Street. *(He switches the cassette player off and looks at the driver.)* Y' goin to flood that engine the way y' going on.

LAWTON. I'm sure there's somethin' wrong with this you know.

He gets the engine to turn over, but has the gears engaged in first. The van jumps forward, but just stops before it crashes into the back of the lorry, mainly because the passenger throws the handbrake on as he jerks forward and hits the windscreen.

MOSS. *(Politely.)* Have you been driving long, Leslie?

LAWTON. No, it's . . . *(He starts the car and discovers the reverse.)* I'm not used to this one, that's all.

MOSS. What was the number of the house Malone came out of?

Lawton crashes gears and pulls forward.

LAWTON. Dunno. But it'll be on record. I've followed him before. The little sod walked me all around town and then lost me in Mothercare.

He rolls into the kerb.

MOSS. Jesus.

LAWTON. No, y'see, I've er got an automatic at home, and it's . . . and it's hard to . . . *(He crashes the gears again.)* . . . get used to the er . . .

MOSS. Look, just get a move on, will y'? They'll be half way down the road by now.

We see inside the van as it slowly reverses.

LAWTON. We're alright – we know where they're going to end up anyway. Malloy's site. If we lose them we just go there.

He crashes the gears yet again and starts off towards the end of the road.

MOSS. Yeah, but it would be nice to see who else they pick up, and where. *(The car mounts the pavement.)* You can use second gear, you know, if you want to. *(Second gear goes in painfully.)* Not that it'll make much difference. All we're doing is catching tadpoles and tiddlers.

The van continues up the road, two wheels on the kerb.

LAWTON. Oh, I wouldn't say that . . .

MOSS. *(Looking out of the window.)* Do you know you've only got two wheels on the kerb? Ever thought about being a stunt driver? Leslie.

The car goes up and down the kerbs.

LAWTON. No.

MOSS. Don't. Y'll only make me cry. Just turn the corner and put your foot down. *(He misses a beat.)* Y' right foot.

The van turns left at the end of the road. The right indicator is flashing. Tyres screech.

11. Interior. Transit. Day.

The Transit van crosses over a bridge. Inside the van, Jimmy and Chrissie are in the front, Loggo and Snowy in the back. Loggo is looking at Snowy's lumps and cuts. He grins at him.

LOGGO. Well then, who was it worked you over this time, Snowy? The boys in blue, the NF, the SPG, the CBI, the SS Fraud Section, the anti-abortion league . . .

SNOWY. Y' don't know what y' talkin' about.

LOGGO. Well tell us, anyway. I know y' dyin' to.

SNOWY. No I'm not. And it wouldn't interest you.

LOGGO. Yes it would, I like fairy stories.

SNOWY. They're not fairy stories, Loggo.

LOGGO. Ah but still, go on, I still want t'know what happened.

SNOWY. *(Primly.)* As a matter of fact, I fell off me moped.

Loggo dissolves with laughter and Jimmy and Chrissie join in.

12. Exterior. Dixie's house. Day.

We see the back of Dixie's house. It is a modern terrace with a small front garden, on the corner of a road. The Transit stops and parks on the corner of the alleyway. Chrissie gets out and goes to the back door. Chrissie knocks, Kevin opens the door. He is wearing a sweat-shirt and trousers and is even more battered than Snowy.

CHRISSIE. Alright Kev? Is y' dad – what's the matter with your face?

KEVIN. Nothin' – compared with me ribs. And me dad's in bed.

Chrissie stares at Kevin for a second or two.

CHRISSIE. But he's supposed to be doin' a couple of days with Malloy.

KEVIN. Someone came for him last night. Twelve-hour nights somewhere. He's just got back.

CHRISSIE. Oh right. *(He half turns.)* You'd better get back to bed as well.

KEVIN. I haven't been yet. They've just let me out the police station.

CHRISSIE. Oh ay. Fightin' were y'?

KEVIN. I wasn't – but they were.

CHRISSIE. The Brookvale gang?

KEVIN. Nah, the Brookvale police.

CHRISSIE. Ah go 'way, Kevin – y' mean the police beat y' up for nothin'?

KEVIN. Nah, it's a pack of lies, Chrissie. I tried to have it off with an elephant.

CHRISSIE. But what for?

Someone beeps the horn in the van. Chrissie looks away as he talks, then looks back.

KEVIN. Nothin'. I just happened to be there, that's all.

CHRISSIE. *(Doubtfully.)* Yeah, well, listen. Tell y' dad I called – I haven't really seen Dixie since, since that cock-up in Middlesbrough – y'know.

Now we see Dixie in a vest, opening the door wider.

DIXIE. Oh yeah. Y' mean when me and Kevin got the sack because of you cowboys. And couldn't get another job? Oh yes, happy days they were, Chrissie. *(He grabs Kevin away.)* Thanks for the memory. Now frig off.

He goes to close the door.

CHRISSIE. Ah come on Dix, we're all in the same boat.

DIXIE. Yeah and you sunk it.

Dixie slams the door in Chrissie's face. Chrissie walks off.

13. Exterior. Road. Day.

We see the Transit driving along the road.

13a. Interior. Transit. Day.

We see the Transit van back on the road. It is just starting off towards the main road.

LOGGO. So why doesn't Dixie want the work?

CHRISSIE. He's got something else on, but he wouldn't work with us anyway after Middlesbrough. I don't think Dixie'll ever forget Middlesbrough. Mind you, neither will I.

JIMMY. Why, what happened in Middlesbrough?

CHRISSIE. *(Glances at Loggo.)* Oh nothin' much. We just lost our life's savin's to doin' a foreigner for two con artists.

LOGGO. Yeah, an' Dixie lost his job, because it was his job to see we were on site with him.

CHRISSIE. Y'know, I would seriously like to bomb Middlesbrough off the face of the earth.

LOGGO. Anyway, I don't know why Dixie's got a cob on with us for. I mean if he'd have been doin' his proper job we'd all still be workin'. In fact when y' come to think of it, it was all Dixie's fault.

Chrissie and Loggo exchange sour smiles.

SNOWY. What about his lad, isn't he havin' any?

CHRISSIE. He's not in any state to. He's been beaten black an' blue. By the police, he reckons. An' for nothin'.

SNOWY. Wel!, that's about par for the course.

CHRISSIE. Ah, come on Snowy. I've heard all those stories, but I don't believe any of it.

13b. Exterior/Interior. Transit. Day.

We see the Transit back on the main road. Snowy is in full passionate flow.

SNOWY. Oh eh, where've y' been all y' life? What were y' doin' durin' the Toxteth riots?

Chrissie doesn't answer.

LOGGO. Well, I was down the supermarket a lot.

SNOWY. The police started that, y' know. 'Come here, Sambo, and suck this truncheon.' That's the main reason Toxteth went up, Chrissie. An' for every feller who dies in a police station an' gets his name in the papers, there's hundreds more who get a quiet little hammerin' down a dark alley an' crawl home to bed. I've been worked over too many times meself not to know that.

LOGGO. Yeah, and I know what they did to y' an' all – they knocked y' brains out.

SNOWY. It's fine by me. You make a joke out of it. But be warned, the way things 're goin' with this Government . . .

No one appears to be listening. Loggo has his paper up, Jimmy is looking out of the side window, and Chrissie is staring at the road.

SNOWY. . . . the swing to the right, tax relief for the rich, redundancies for the poor, mass unemployment, poverty, the curtailing of freedom startin' with the unions. It's all headin' for one thing – and one thing only – a fascist dictatorship and a police state!

JIMMY. That's two things.

LOGGO. And it sounds just like Russia, Snowy.

SNOWY. Oh don't be—

LOGGO. Y'know you – you're an offence under the Noise Abatement Act.

SNOWY. *(Looks out of the window.)* All right, all right. But you give it eighteen months and . . . *(He sees something. And sees what he wants to see.)* Look, see, there y'are. The bloody law, and who've they got, eh? Two workin' lads.

> *(We see from their point of view the Marina van. The men are just getting out, and two policemen are getting out of their Rover 3500.)*

Probably nothin' concrete to stop them for, just a bit of harassment, but that's how it starts.

14. Exterior. Dual carriageway traffic lights. Day.

We see the Marina van and the police car. Lawton is facing the two policemen. One of the policemen is very very big.

POLICEMAN. Forty-eight miles an hour in a built-up area.

SNOWY. *(Shouting out of the window of the Transit.)* Bastards!

> *Moss and Lawton look at each other. The policeman glances at the Transit and goes to look away. But then he double-takes and grins as he sees the Transit come to a halt in the rush-hour traffic jam. He turns back to Moss and Lawton.*

POLICEMAN. Wait there. *(He goes.)*

LAWTON. Where did they come from?

> *The policeman walks across the dual carriageway and then along to where the Transit is marooned. He gets to the back doors and opens them. He looks inside, stone-faced.*

POLICEMAN. Who said that?

> *No one will look at him. They all point to Snowy. Then Snowy mumbles.*

SNOWY. It was me.

POLICEMAN. Get out here. Now.

Snowy gets out. The policeman towers over him by at least a foot and a quarter.

Tell me what you said again. Go on. What did you say?

SNOWY. 'Bastard'.

The policeman goes down almost on his haunches to face Snowy.

POLICEMAN. Midget.

The policeman rubs Snowy's head affably, then turns and goes back across the road. As he goes, Chrissie and the others let their laughter out. Snowy goes to get back in the van. He mutters as he goes.

SNOWY. So . . . so. I can't help it. It's not my fault I was a premature baby . . .

We see the policeman arriving back. His colleague shows him an opened wallet with an authorized picture of Lawton inside. He also has Lawton begins to protest.

POLICEMAN. Well, well, well, Geoffrey. We are honoured. Two sniffers from the dole. *(He looks them up and down.)*

LAWTON. I wouldn't quite put it like that, but it . . .

POLICEMAN. Takes a good picture, doesn't he?

LAWTON. Look. We are right in the middle of a very important investigation.

As Lawton talks, the second policeman passes his licence over.

POLICEMAN. *(He walks to the car.)* Ooh, who's a naughty boy then? *(He looks at the front of the Marina.)* Hey? Exceeding the speed limits, driving in a manner likely to cause an accident . . .

Lawton begins to protest.

LAWTON. Come on . . .

POLICEMAN. *(Crushing Lawton's protest.)* . . . and then just for luck, no 'L' plates on display.

The policeman tut-tuts. Moss shakes his head in total disbelief. The policeman starts writing the ticket as he talks.

POLICEMAN. I hope for your sake, Mr . . . Lawton, your passenger has a licence. A full licence.

LAWTON. Look, er . . .

POLICEMAN. Not like your one.

Moss takes out his wallet. Removes his driving licence and displays it for the policeman. Lawton dribbles on.

LAWTON. *(He walks to the police car.)* You know, we work very closely with some of your boys, and we . . .

POLICEMAN. *(Withering him.)* Insurance?

The second policeman walks to the police car and gets in.

LAWTON. I expect it's . . . er it's . . .

POLICEMAN. Produce your insurance document at your nearest police station within the next five days. If you would be so kind. *(He gives Lawton the ticket.)* I was on the dole for eighteen months, friend. That's why I'm here today giving you a ticket. 'Cos I've met your kind before. *(He turns away.)* Have a nice day. *(He gets in.)*

The police car drives away. We see Lawton looking at them and then sneaking a look at Moss.

LAWTON. I didn't like his tone, y'know. I've got a good mind . . .

MOSS. Get in. *(Moss pushes him towards the passenger side of the van.)*

LAWTON. I just thought, y'know, I'd put a bit of practice in. Me test's comin' up in a fortnight and I thought with having this job . . . *(He climbs into the van as he talks.)*

MOSS. Oh yeah all right, and you thought with me being new here, a woolly-back from Wigan, you could . . .

LAWTON. Oh Donald, believe me . . .

MOSS. *(As he starts the van up and moves away.)* Just shut up, will you . . . We'd better go back and get this van changed. I don't know who they were calling bastards, but they're sure to have clocked us in this.

LAWTON. I'm sorry, Donald, I am, really. *(He coughs.)* You won't tell anyone, will you?

   The Marina van drives off.

15.   Exterior. Malloy's site. Day.

Malloy's site is a former bridewell. We see the Transit driving into the courtyard of the bridewell so that it is out of sight of the roadway. The van parks and the men get out and approach the site hut.

15a.   Interior. Site Hut. Day.

Snowy opens the hut door, and as the men stand at the entrance, we see the interior in shadows. In the shadows furthest from the door is a figure. As the light comes in from the doorway, we see it is George, dressed as he was before, but now he is enveloped in a pair of trousers several quietly ludicrous sizes too big for him. Snowy opens the door fully, sees his father and says sadly:

SNOWY. Oh no. Not again, dad.

GEORGE. Chrissie told me y' were here.

CHRISSIE. But I didn't tell y' to turn up.

SNOWY. *(Entering the hut.)* Come 'head, I'll take you back. *(Snowy brings George out.)*

GEORGE. I'm only across the road, lad, and I mean I'm doin'

nothin'. Besides I thought y' might have been short-handed. You know, son.

CHRISSIE. Course y' did, but we're all right. Come on we'll take y' back. *(He turns to Loggo.)* Get a brew on Loggo, will you, we won't be long.

Loggo and Jimmy go into the site hut while Chrissie and Snowy lead George away from it.

15b. Exterior. Malloy's site. Day.

We see George with Snowy and Chrissie linking him, moving slowly away from the site hut through the archway to the road and the Royal Hospital.

SNOWY. Where did y' get the trousers?

GEORGE. I borrowed them, Michael.

SNOWY. Off the giant in the next bed?

GEORGE. Next bed but one. Those two miserable sods on either side wouldn't lend me theirs. Why worry? I'm getting transferred from here to Walton Hospital. At an undisclosed fee.

SNOWY. What are we goin' to do with you, dad?

GEORGE. How about giving me a job as a can lad? I could do that as a start.

16. Interior. Site Hut. Day.

The site hut interior reveals the normal dismal site hut/workman's room. There are a few old chairs, a bench, a few nudes on the wall alongside an architect's drawing, a Calor Gas heater, a small hob and a kettle. The floor is littered with screwed-up chip papers and old newspapers. A bottle of sterilized milk and a few extremely dirty cups stand on the table. The men are sitting on benches. The kettle has just boiled and Chrissie and Snowy have just returned. As Chrissie is nearest the kettle he is about to be mother.

SNOWY. Well yeah, there is a bit of work f'plasterers at the moment.

He leaves it at that, he waits for the next inevitable question with a certain pride. Chrissie begins to pour the water from the kettle into the brew can.

JIMMY. So what are y' doin' here then on fourteen pound a day?

SNOWY. I'm blacklisted.

JIMMY. What for?

SNOWY. I start strikes.

LOGGO. Not a bad reason.

SNOWY. And I'm also in the WRP.

CHRISSIE. *(Winking at the others behind Snowy's back.)* Didn't they use to have them during the war – y'know, tin hats an' gas masks an' knock at y' door if y' haven't drawn y' curtains?

SNOWY. The Workers' Revolutionary Party.

JIMMY. Oh aye. I remember them. They were at our factory gates the day we closed down. Full of brotherly love and fight the good fight an' all that. We still closed down.

LOGGO. Yeah. But Snowy's different, aren't y', Snowy? Not the same as all those others in that there . . . 'Workers' Revolutionary Party' . . . Right that, isn't it? Y' the only one who's workin' class.

SNOWY. I can take it y'know, Loggo. I can take it 'cos I know my beliefs are right. I've been brought up by me dad to support what's worth supportin'—

LOGGO. I didn't know y' dad followed Everton.

SNOWY. All I'm saying is, if y' don't fight, if y' know, if . . . like I mean, it was easy to be a socialist when I was growin' up in the sixties, an' even f'most of the seventies. Everyone was a friggin' socialist then. It was fashionable. But it's not now . . . Everythin's gone sour, everyone's lockin' the door, turnin' the other cheek, lookin' after number one. *But now's the time when we should all be together.* Now's the time when we *need* to be together, 'cos . . . 'cos well we're not winnin' anymore. *Don't you see that? (He pauses.)* Like, that's all I'm sayin'.

CHRISSIE. *(Gently.)* Of course we see it.

JIMMY. And the last thing we need is t'be told about it, f'Christ's sake.

CHRISSIE. 'Cos deep down, most of us know it. But y' don't look that far, not these days. Not when y' scared Snowy. And when y' scared, unless y' very special, y' think about y'self – an' yours. Y' think about feedin' the kids, an' payin' the rent, an' the effect it's havin' on y' tart – an' even what Christmas is going to be like this year. *(He shrugs.)* I'm a married man with two kids, an' y'beliefs go right out of the window when y' debtors knock at your door. *(There is a pause.)* And what's more I shouldn't be here now. The sniffers've been round our house twice this past fortnight.

SNOWY. But y' need the money.

CHRISSIE. Got it in one.

SNOWY. *(Shaking his head.)* I know – I need it too.

JIMMY. Is there no chance of a start with Malloy?

CHRISSIE. Yeah, well, that's what I want to know an' all. I did a couple of days for him last week. Asked him then, but he sort of avoided it. I've only come today so I can ask him again.

JIMMY. Do you know what? I would do anythin' if I thought . . .

SNOWY. What did you used to be Jimmy?

JIMMY. I used to be a machine fitter, *an' I still am.*

Snowy looks embarrassed.

SNOWY. Frig . . . sorry.

CHRISSIE. He's here now.

We see Malloy. Chrissie opens the door and goes.

JIMMY. What time is it?

LOGGO. *(Flashing his watch.)* Oh it's about twenty minutes after
we should have started work . . .

Loggo and Jimmy move towards the doorway.

SNOWY. Hey – *Hey*! Hang about. Look at the state of y' –
panickin' just because the boss is here, jumpin' up an' runnin'.
Y'll be touchin' y' forelocks next. *(As he talks, he picks up his two
lengths of rope and approaches the others near the door.)* Let's not
make it so obvious, hey? Right? Okay, let's go!

He races for the door and gets there first. Laughter as they go.

17. Exterior. Malloy's site. Day.

*Malloy is in wellies and a tweed suit. He is a quietly affluent,
overweight Irishman in his late forties. He should give the impression of
being able to handle himself once. As the lads walk up from the site hut,
he glances at his watch, but without threat. The lads approach him.*

MALLOY. One short then are we?

LOGGO. Well y' know what it's like. First sign of Spring an' all
the boys are off to Spain – I mean, after all it's a shame to let
the villas go to waste.

MALLOY. *(Grinning.)* And who are you when you're out?

LOGGO. I am *the* brickie. That's how I served my time. It was
some time ago but . . .

CHRISSIE. We did have another brickie but he got a proper job.

Snowy puts the ropes on his shoulder.

MALLOY. Well. That's good to hear – anyway . . . see y've
brought your ropes, Snowy? *(He laughs to himself.)* But I don't
think they'll come looking for you here, though.

SNOWY. This used to be a bridwell, didn't it?

Malloy nods.

It's not goin' to be a police station again, is it – 'cos y'know, I do have certain moral objections to working . . .

MALLOY. Nah; it's not going to be that. But you could say it was another growth industry. One of the few. Okay, I can leave you on your own now, can't I?

SNOWY. *(Turning back.)* I'll need someone to mix for me every so often.

MALLOY. Kenny'll do that.

CHRISSIE. *(To Snowy.)* Kenny won't, but Chrissie might.

Snowy grins and moves back into the yard to go upstairs with his ropes. He will go to the room he is plastering first.

MALLOY. You're not a brickie, are you, by any chance?

Jimmy hestitates slightly, then shakes his head.

JIMMY. Sorry.

MALLOY. Don't worry. There's still some landscapin' needs doing . . . that patch over there. Flatten the hump out, pick out all the half sets and rubble and that should . . . that should . . .

Malloy has just seen Yosser and his children. Yosser is walking down from a low hill towards them, through the mud, with his three children in tow. He is walking with the air of a man with total confidence in his own destiny. He appears to know where he is going, even if no one else does.

CHRISSIE. *(To Loggo, quietly.)* Look what's coming.

LOGGO. Oh frig.

They turn away. Yosser arrives. Loggo and Chrissie are looking at him. Only Jimmy is looking at Malloy, who is looking at Yosser.

YOSSER. *(Smiling, speaking rapidly.)* Gizza job, go on, gizzit, go 'head

MALLOY. A job? *(He looks at Yosser's children.)*

YOSSER. Yeah, gizzit, go on, I know you've got one, Arthur told me, go on, gizzit.

MALLOY. Now? Today? Well what about the . . . *(He points at the kids.)*

YOSSER. Oh yeah. Oh aye, yeah. Oh too right, yeah. *(He takes his coat off.)* I'm ready.

MALLOY. I only need a brickie.

YOSSER. Yis, that's me. I'm a brickie. I can lay bricks.

(We see Loggo and Chrissie look at each other.)

MALLOY. Well there's er . . . there's . . . that small wall runnin' parallel with the one that he's going to be workin' on.

(Yosser grabs Loggo's tool bag and is already on his way.)

I'll see how you . . . how you make out on . . . *(He is talking to himself. He looks at Yosser then at the others.)* . . . trial basis . . . Do you know him?

LOGGO. We used to.

Loggo walks away towards the two parallel walls. Jimmy goes towards the rubble-strewn landscape. Malloy turns away from Chrissie in the archway and goes towards his car which is parked just around the corner of the building. Chrissie walks with him.

CHRISSIE. . . . How's the new site going, Mr Malloy?

MALLOY. Fine, just fine.

As Malloy speaks, we see the first length of rope drop to the ground, right in front of them. They both look up. Snowy grins down at them, before he pops his head back in. They carry on walking and talking.

CHRISSIE. Y' busy then are y'?

MALLOY. *(Glancing at him.)* Not really, not for the time of the year. And not after the winter we had.

CHRISSIE. Y' never know, though, we might have a good summer.

MALLOY. Still die off once the bad weather comes back. Always does.

CHRISSIE. I was just wonderin' Mr Malloy.

They have reached the car. Malloy begins to climb in it.

MALLOY. I'm sorry Kenny, but . . .

CHRISSIE. Chrissie.

MALLOY. Yeah, Chrissie. *(He turns the engine over.)*

CHRISSIE. Nevertheless, Mr Malloy, I mean it could be a couple of months before the weather changes.

MALLOY. Look, I've really got to dash, y'know how it is.

He is moving the car forward, away from the building, towards the side of a three-storey building.

CHRISSIE. *(Running with him.)* I only want a few words if—

MALLOY. I'll be back before dinner, to see how our friend the mad brickie's shapin' up. Speak to me then.

Malloy spurts away in the car. Chrissie walks towards the wall of the three-storey section and watches Malloy go. Another rope cascades down at his side. Chrissie glances up and sees Snowy.

SNOWY. You know the score, Chrissie - there's nothin' down for y'. That's the way it is and that's the way it will be until we—

Chrissie moves away from the building to look up and glare at him, knowing that another piece of politics is on the way down.

SNOWY. Best not to think about it, if it hurts that much.

CHRISSIE. *(Bitterly.)* Yeah, well. We'll see about that.

Snowy starts to pull in his rope. Chrissie turns and kicks out at a bag of masonry cement. The bag rips and spurts. Chrissie walks away.

18.   Interior. Snowy's room. Day.

We see the room where Snowy is plastering. One door leads to a

*corridor. Two windows face out towards the parallel walls. Each window
is large enough for a man to climb through. Snowy's rope is attached to
and wrapped around a radiator, and then to the window frame, before
dropping out of the window. Snowy is plastering feverishly, whistling. He
has the appearance and energy of a little man doing a big job, and doing
it very well. Chrissie is in the centre of the room, standing by the board
full of plaster he has just mixed for Snowy. He walks to the window and
wipes his hands.*

SNOWY. *(Whistling, looks around as he works.)* Thanks Chrissie.

   (No reaction.)

Y'alright?

   Chrissie nods and walks to the centre of the room.

I'll probably need another mix in a few minutes.

CHRISSIE. *(Still without turning.)* You'll be lucky. It's nearly
dinnertime now.

SNOWY. It's not is it? Jeezus, doesn't time fly when y 'havin'
fun.

   *He laughs and looks at Chrissie. No reaction again. Then Snowy
talks as he continues to work.*

SNOWY. I love doin' this, y'know.

CHRISSIE. Yeah, I've noticed.

SNOWY. I'd plaster f'nothing if me principles'd let me – know
what I mean?

CHRISSIE. Not off-hand, Snowy, no.

SNOWY. Y'know, doin' somethin' y' good at – there's nothin'
like it. Standin' there in the mornin' facin' four empty walls –
an' then goin' home at night with the plaster all dry and
smooth – an' the bit y've just done all wet an' shinin' . . . That's
why I don't mind workin' on me own, if the truth be told, 'cos
if there's one thing I can't stand, it's workin' with someone who
hasn't got no pride . . . An' funny enough, they're the kind that
never want to come out on strike. No pride *and* no principles.

   Chrissie continues to stare out of the window.

Like some of the sods who've renovated this place. Have y' seen
it – it's shoddy already – half the wood's warped, there's a fall in the
floor and a leak on the landin'. Nothin'll last here – except the
building itself, and the plaster on the walls . . . Y' wanna see
somethin'? *(Walks to the centre, stops and looks at Chrissie.)* Hey
Chrissie – come here.

CHRISSIE. *(Turning to Snowy.)* Do I have to?

    *Chrissie looks at Snowy, shrugs and half-grins. Snowy walks to the
door.*

SNOWY. No, I want to show you something. It won't take long.
(He tests the plaster on the wall.) An' that'll hold for a while.

18a.   Exterior. Malloy's site. Day.

*Jimmy Johnson is 'landscaping'. He is being helped by Yosser's eldest
boy as they pick out the most obvious half sets and big stones. They have
their backs turned to where they are piling the stones.*

JIMMY. Hey. You can come again, kidder. Keep this up an' I might
just increase your non-taxable allowance to ten p. an hour. *He smiles.)*
You can't drive a JCB by any chance can you?

    *Suddenly we hear the thud of stone against bucket. They turn back
with a handful of bricks and stones each, and look towards where they
have piled the stones and bricks already gathered. They see Yosser's
youngest child busy throwing them all over the place again with gay
abandon. Jimmy sags visibly, and begins to walk over.*

JIMMY. What do you think you're doing you little . . . do you
think I'm carrying these bricks round for the good of my
health? Come on, get them up!

    *As he walks over, we see in the foreground Loggo and Yosser crouched
over their respective walls. But we cannot make out clearly the quality
of their walls.*

LOGGO. Eh Yosser . . . Yosser . . . *Yosser* . . . y' can't leave gaps
like that.

YOSSER. It's for ventilation.

LOGGO. *(He sighs.)* Oh Christ . . .

18b. Interior. Corridor of third-floor.

Chrissie and Snowy are walking along the corridor.

SNOWY. You see . . .

> *Snowy touches the tiles. Chrissie looks at Snowy and then at the tiles on the wall.*

CHRISSIE. It's a tile, Snowy. Lots of tiles. Brown ones.

SNOWY. Yeah, I know, I know, nothin' special. Just beautifully made and precision laid a hundred years ago – and still like new. Apart from those that've been cracked to buggery by the idiot who put the new banister up.

> *The rope is hanging out attached to a window frame and the banister, running down the steps leading to the cells. Snowy touches the tiles again, and the finish. Chrissie looks at him as he walks out to the landing.*

CHRISSIE. Is that it? Can I go now?

> *They lift the rope on the landing and walk under.*

SNOWY. But don't y'see—

> *Chrissie turns away, without insult, and moves towards the door leading onto the flat roof.*

18c. Exterior. Flat roof, Malloy's site.

They walk across the roof, back towards where Snowy was plastering.

SNOWY. We're all capable of work like that. Craftsmanship doesn't die out in people, Chrissie. We can all do good jobs, but we're not allowed to. I don't get jobs just because of me politics, y'know.

> *Chrissie glances at him.*

There's times when I'm not taken on because I'm too good. And because I'm good, and I do the job proper, I refuse to skimp on the stuff and I'm slower than the bosses want me to be. And then I'm not a profit margin anymore, I'm a liability.

CHRISSIE. *(Gently, as he puts his arm round Snowy.)* Do y' ever lose any work because y' talk too much?

SNOWY. *(With disarming sincerity.)* All right. But listen Chrissie, I'm tellin' you, an' I mean it, don't give in, 'cos if y' give in, y' dead. An' I'm only tellin' y' 'cos I can see the signs.

Chrissie hugs him like a brother and pushes him towards the door.

CHRISSIE. Get in.

They go inside the doorway.

18d. Interior. Snowy's room. Day.

Chrissie and Snowy enter the room. While Snowy looks at his wall, Chrissie goes to the window and looks out. Snowy admires the wall he is plastering and the wall opposite the fireplace.

SNOWY. *(Lightly.)* Oh hey. Would you look at that? Just look at that. Sometimes, y' know . . . *(Almost shyly.)* . . . Sometimes I'm so proud of what I've done, I put me name on the bottom right-hand corner of the wall . . . 'Snowy Malone, 1982.' *(He pauses.)* Y'know, Chrissie, thinkin' about it, the job with Malloy . . .

CHRISSIE. *I know.* And I wasn't thinkin' about it just then.

SNOWY. Oh . . . Still bad down there?

CHRISSIE. Bad? That's a compliment.

Chrissie looks at Snowy and indicates out of the window. Snowy comes forward and looks out.

19. Exterior. Malloy's site.

Snowy and Chrissie are looking out at Yosser at his wall, which leads out from the building, no more than two-thirds of a metre in height. The wall meanders from the string line, bricks stick out at odd angles, there is the occasional 'ventilation' gap between bricks, and the cement sticks out from between the bricks. It is, however, a long wall and Yosser is manically making it longer by the second. Loggo is going along straight and steady on his wall leading from the building, providing a perfect contrast. We also see Yosser's daughter handing him each brick to put into the wall as he goes wildly on. We hear Chrissie and Snowy as we see these sights.

CHRISSIE. He's off his cake, Snowy. Everytime I've seen him since he was with us in Middlesbrough he's just got . . . worse. An' the stories y' hear.

SNOWY. Been to see me dad, y'know. Yeah, just turned up one night, sat there with him for nearly an hour, starin' at me dad. Nurse had to ask him to go in the end. When he started cryin'.

20. Interior. Snowy's room. Day.

Chrissie and Snowy are still at the window.

CHRISSIE. When who started cryin'?

SNOWY. Yosser.

CHRISSIE. Kinnell . . .

There is a pause.

SNOWY. Y'd better tell him about that.

CHRISSIE. I already have done. So's Loggo.

SNOWY. Y'll have to tell him again, then.

CHRISSIE. For all the good it'll do. It's like talkin' to a brick wall.

He smiles slightly as he realizes what he has said.

21. Exterior. Malloy's site. Day.

Yosser carries a spadeful of cement. Chrissie runs after him. We see the brick wall. We see Yosser slamming another brick, neither into line nor place. He is bent over, back turned, covered in sand and cement. Chrissie and Loggo are alongside him.

CHRISSIE. But . . . but Yosser, y' don't know what y' doin'. *(No answer.)* He'll go spare when he comes back. *(No answer.)* Yosser! *(No answer.)*

LOGGO. Look! Tell y' what, Yos, you work the hod for a while hey, I'll lay the bricks, work a tandem.

There is still no answer. Chrissie looks at the brickwork in despair. He bends onto his haunches. Chrissie stops Yosser and points out one of his worst efforts.

CHRISSIE. Look Yos, that one's not even—

YOSSER. Leave my wall alone.

He knocks Chrissie's hand away with the trowel, stares at Chrissie and then smiles, wild and warm, before throwing another brick into the wall. Chrissie gives up, stands up and moves away.

CHRISSIE. Come on . . . it's dinnertime.

As Loggo and Chrissie move away and Yosser goes too, a green Marina van goes past the site on the road above, slightly slower than would be expected. It comes to a halt further along the road.

22. Exterior. Road outside Malloy's site. Day.

The green Marina van stops almost out of sight of the site. Moss is now driving, while Lawton is the passenger.

MOSS. . . . It's a Mercedes, Leslie. I'm no connoisseur, but I know a Mercedes when I see one.

LAWTON. *(Looking down at the file on his knee.)* All I'm saying is—

MOSS. You saw him in it yourself at his other site.

LAWTON. All I'm sayin' is that it says here it's a green 'T'-reg Ford Granada. Obviously he must have changed his car.

MOSS. No manners have they some people? Y' would've thought he'd have had the decency to let us know.

They turn to see a boy go by. Yosser's eldest lad scampers past them with a parcel of chips, and goes down towards the site. Lawton contemplates reacting to Moss's sarcasm, but thinks better of it. Moss looks up, nudges Lawton and indicates as he sees the Mercedes followed by a council wagon go past towards the site entrance. Moss smiles and starts to unpack his lunch.

LAWTON. . . . Still, when you think about it, it's a good job we had to take that other van back.

Moss stares dolefully at him for a second or so.

MOSS. Aye . . . That's what your superiors are for – to keep you completely in the dark. Particularly our delightful boss – living proof of the folly of female emancipation. Knowin' her, she wouldn't have told us what was goin' to happen.

LAWTON.   It wouldn't be the first time, Donald.

MOSS. Don't I know it. Do you know I followed a bloke to court one morning last month and sat there and watched while he went to the dock and pleaded guilty to the offences I was still following him for? *(He looks at Lawton.)* I'd been on sick leave when they pulled him in, but nobody thought to let me know when I came back.

He turns right around, to look back through the window down towards the building site. The Mercedes and the council wagon pull up in front of the bridewell.

LAWTON. *(He turns.)* Well, at least *something's* happening. Won't be long now . . . He's got a nerve though, hasn't he, this Malloy character?

MOSS. You mean having lads here? I'll say.

Moss smiles and then laughs.

23. Exterior. Malloy's site. Day.

By the entrance leading into the inner yard, Malloy is getting out of his car which is parked on the corner to give access to the wagon. Malloy only has eyes for the wall which he is walking towards, staring.

COUNCIL WORKER. Where's the sign goin', feller?

MALLOY. . . . What er, oh yeah . . . up there, over the . . . entrance.

Malloy walks around the brickwork, and stops with his hand over his mouth. He looks again, still unable to believe it. We hear the council worker, talking to his driver.

COUNCIL WORKER. Take the wagon in the yard, Phil and stand on the back to put it up.

Malloy glances up at them as they move the wagon into the yard, so that only the very tail of the wagon is sticking out. He finally manages to drag himself away from the freewheeling brickwork and moves towards the site hut, inside the yard.

24. Interior. Site hut. Day.

Inside the site hut, all the men, except Yosser, have got some kind of carrying out. A brew is on. Snowy is starting a joke. Yosser is sitting away from the others on the floor against the far wall with his kids and chips. He is sharing the chips out.

SNOWY. . . . I'm havin' terrible trouble sleepin', y'know. It's the dole that does it, though, isn't it? Went to the doctor's last week, told him straight – 'I'm on the dole, doctor, an' I can't sleep'. So fair enough, he told me to take these pills of a night before I went to bed – but I told him goin' to sleep at night wasn't the trouble. So he suggested that when I woke up in the early hours of the mornin', I take one so that I can get me head down again. But I told him that wasn't no trouble neither, so he got a bit ratty with me then, and asked me when it was I couldn't sleep. An' I told him—

Everyone except Yosser joins in on the punchline. Quietly and almost lethargically.

ALL. 'It's the afternoons.'

SNOWY. Ah, y've heard it . . .

Malloy enters. The lads look up and then away. They move to let Malloy through. Malloy makes his way towards Yosser, stands over him and the kids and then speaks quietly.

MALLOY. You do that wall?

YOSSER. *(Looking up as he claws chips into his mouth.)* What wall?

MALLOY. The wall I asked y' to do.

YOSSER. Yeah, what about it? *(More chips.)*

MALLOY. Come and take a look at it.

YOSSER. I've seen it. *(He laughs.)* Once you've seen one wall, y've seen them all. *(He laughs again, and looks at the others.)*

MALLOY. Not this one. This is special.

YOSSER. Good hey? *(He looks around again.)*

MALLOY. Come and see it again. It's well worth seeing twice. *(He turns away and goes towards the door, then stops and looks back.)* Now.

YOSSER. Don't tell me what to do. Nobody tells me what to do.

But Yosser stands up and follows Malloy, stomps past Chrissie and out of the door, ignoring Chrissie's speech.

CHRISSIE. Take it easy, eh, Yosser? I want a word with . . .

Yosser goes out, followed by his kids.

LOGGO. Well, Chrissie. Y'can always have a cosy little chat while y' walkin' him over to Casualty . . . *(Loggo gets up as he talks and goes to follow Malloy and Yosser.)*

Chrissie, Jimmy and Snowy follow him out of the hut.

25.   **Exterior. Malloy's site. Day.**

Yosser is standing by the wall with Malloy. The kids are a few yards away. Snowy, Loggo, Chrissie and Jimmy are leaning against the wall by the wagon. They watch from afar. The council men are on top of the back of the wagon drilling holes in the brickwork to support the sign as this goes on.

MALLOY. But what were you doing, man?

YOSSER. I was doin' my best.

MALLOY. Your best? That can't be your best – that's a disgrace. *(He prods at the wall with his toe.)*

YOSSER. *(Quietly.)* Leave my wall alone.

MALLOY. But look at it.

YOSSER. Last for ever, that.

MALLOY. *(Laughing at him.)* I know one thing – you're not a brickie.

YOSSER. I am.

MALLOY. You're not. Y' can't be – not if that's your best.

YOSSER. I've laid bricks before. Anyone can lay bricks.

MALLOY. Listen son, the last time you laid bricks was when you had a Lego set. *(He reaches for his inside pocket for his wallet to pay Yosser off as Yosser leans back to butt him.)* You're no good to me.

Yosser butts him and lays him flat and over the wall. The lads come forward. Malloy gets up, puts his fists up and tries to hit Yosser. Yosser grabs his fist, and speaks sanely and soberly.

YOSSER. I wouldn't do that if I were you. 'Cos if y' do, I'll kill y'.

As they face each other, the two council men stop and look from the top of their wagon.

MALLOY. Go on, clear off – you're sacked.

YOSSER. *(Laughing.) Me* – sacked? *(Laughs again.)* How can y' sack someone who's on the dole? *(Still laughing, he walks to the others. His children follow him.)* He's sacked me, boys, he's sacked a man who doesn't even work for him. *(He laughs.)* I'll tell y' somethin' – he'll have trouble findin' me P45.

He walks off, kicks his wall over and strides away confidently as the kids run after him. Chrissie watches him go.

26.   Interior. Site hut. Day.

Inside the hut, Malloy is sitting on a chair slightly away from the table and the others. His nose has stopped bleeding but is puffed up. Loggo and Jimmy are reading their papers, Chrissie and Snowy just finishing off their cups of tea. Silence.

SNOWY. . . . Want another cup of tea?

MALLOY. No, no, I can hardly finish this one. Anyway, I've got to go. *(He stands up and looks at them.)* And so have you. *(Tries to smile as they look up at him.)* Back to work.

He waits till they make a move towards the doorway. Chrissie doesn't stand up. Snowy watches him, tries to catch his eye. Chrissie looks away. Snowy talks to Chrissie.

SNOWY. How are you fixed for some more mixin'? Won't take a minute.

CHRISSIE. An' I won't be a minute.

Chrissie stays where he is. Snowy goes and closes the door. Malloy sits. Both speak together.

MALLOY. If y'—

CHRISSIE. I was—

MALLOY. Go on.

CHRISSIE. No, no. You.

MALLOY. *(Sits down.)* Well, I've got nothing to say. It was you wanted to speak to me.

CHRISSIE. Yeah, well I was . . . I'm not happy at the way things are now, Mr Malloy, fourteen pound a day and . . .

MALLOY. In y' hand.

CHRISSIE. Yeah I know, it's all well an' good but it's not legal an' things are bad for me down the dole, an' what I'm sayin' is I want a job. I want a proper job. This is no use to me.

MALLOY. Isn't it more use than no job at all?

CHRISSIE. You don't want to take me on?

MALLOY. It's not a question of that.

CHRISSIE. I know I'm losing money asking you this, but I'd rather be legit on a lot less. *I wanna be a working man again.* I wanna come home at night with dirt on me hands and not have to hide it from anybody.

MALLOY. If you would just listen to me for a minute, Kenny—

CHRISSIE. You don't want to take me on? Right, fine.

Chrissie gets up and starts packing his stuff into his bag. He collects his paper and tools.

MALLOY. If I took you on, what would happen the weeks when there was no work, when the winter comes again, when I'd have to find your weekly wage so you could play cards, drink tea and piss in the snow? What do you want me to do – take you on for a few months and then lay you off when there's frost on the ground, like the big firms do? Hey? What do you want, promises or the truth, Kenny?

CHRISSIE. *(He stops what he is doing.)* I wouldn't mind me real name. *(He has his anorak on.)*

MALLOY. Yeah. Chrissie.

CHRISSIE. That's right, Chrissie. Y' can remember it when I'm gone.

Malloy gets up and goes to the back of the hut.

MALLOY. You're not listening to a word I'm saying. Look, this is the building game, this is Britain in 1982.
It's . . . just . . . not . . . worth . . . my while.

Chrissie heads for the door.

Where are you going?

CHRISSIE. Home. *(He is now at the door.)*

MALLOY. *(Calmly.)* Can any of the others drive?

CHRISSIE. No. *(He opens the door, and goes out followed by Malloy.)*

MALLOY. What about the van?

CHRISSIE. Snowy can handle a moped. Sometimes.

MALLOY. *(Deliberately. Flatly).* But what am I goin' to do?

CHRISSIE. Don't ask me. I don't work for you. Remember?

MALLOY. *(Friendly.)* Okay, don't worry, I'll find someone. *(He goes for his wallet again.)* Here, here's a five f' —

CHRISSIE. Frig off, Malloy, I don't need charity. Give it to Oxfam. *(He goes to walk off, but stops.)* I used t'be soft, y' know, noted for it. But not anymore. I've had it up to here.

Chrissie indicates his forehead.

27. Exterior. Road outside Malloy's site. Day.

Moss and Lawton are in the green Marina. Lawton is playing with a Rubik Cube. Moss is cleaning his glasses. He looks in the mirror and turns to look out as two similar vans come quickly towards the back of their van, both tooting and flashing their lights as they approach. Moss sits up, turns the ignition on, revs up and throws the van expertly into first gear. Lawton is still jerked forward however.

MOSS. Sods, they're going to beat us to it. Put that bloody thing away. Jesus Christ!

LAWTON. Has something upset you?

They approach the site.

28. Exterior. Malloy's site. Day.

The council workmen are packing up their ladder. We hear laughter.

LOGGO. Jimmy, I don't believe it.

JIMMY. Hang on, where's Chrissie.

Chrissie appears through the gap between the wall and the wagon. Loggo sees Chrissie, goes towards him and grabs hold of him. Loggo pulls Chrissie away from the entrance.

LOGGO. Come here, Chrissie, come on over here . . .

CHRISSIE. What for?

LOGGO. Never you mind.

CHRISSIE. Oh hey.

LOGGO. No y'll like this.

Loggo positions Chrissie with his back turned to the sign above, the entrance, a few yards away from it. Loggo goes behind Chrissie, puts his hands over Chrissie's eyes and turns him around as he talks.

LOGGO. Now turn around.

CHRISSIE. I'm not in the mood, Loggo.

LOGGO. Y' will be. Now think hard, what would y' say this is?

CHRISSIE. Wha'?

LOGGO. What do you reckon this buildin' is going to be, eh? This former cop-shop.

CHRISSIE. I don't know, do I?

LOGGO. Well have one guess.

CHRISSIE. Oh look. Stop friggin' about.

LOGGO. Do you give in then?

CHRISSIE. Yeah, yeah, yeah. I give in.

LOGGO. *(Imitating a fanfare.)* Der der der der! der der der der! der der der der der! Can you believe it! Look!

Loggo takes his hands away. Chrissie is standing in front of the newly erected sign. And we see for the first time that the sign indicates that the building is going to be an unemployment office.

LOGGO. Can you believe that? Can you believe that?

Chrissie looks at Loggo and Jimmy. He grins and giggles. All three rapidly begin to roar with laughter.

Malloy is standing by his car, watching, laughing.

29.   Interior. Snowy's room. Day.

*Snowy is still in the room that he is plastering. He is on his haunches
by the bottom right hand corner of the wall he has just completed. He is
putting his name and the year in tiny writing in the corner with a pocket
screwdriver. He hears the laughter from the others coming through the
window. They are still out of view.*

LOGGO. Snowy'll do his bleedin' nut when he sees that.

CHRISSIE. Get him down here.

LOGGO. He'll love this.

*Snowy stops and goes towards the window. He looks down and sees
the lads, plus Malloy just starting his three-point turn.*

CHRISSIE. Snowy!

LOGGO. Snowy, hey, come 'head, come here!

30.   Exterior. Malloy's site. Day.

From the outside we see Snowy looking down.

SNOWY. What's the matter?

LOGGO. *(Still sniggering.)* Come here and we'll show y'. Come
'head.

We see Snowy turn away from the window.

31.   Exterior. Malloy's site. Day.

*We see the following events. The three green vans turn into the site at
some speed, aiming to get past the building and block the men's escape
onto the main road and up the low hill or towards the hospital. Malloy
is doing a three-point turn. Loggo spots the vans arriving and grabs
Chrissie, and the pair of them grab Jimmy and shout towards the
building. They start to run towards the roadway where the green Marina
was. Malloy drives up behind. However, the first van rams straight into
the council wagon as it reverses happily out of the entrance to the yard.*

*And the second van hits the back of the first one. and the green van
slithers and skids sideways into the second van. For a split second we see
Lawton smirking at Moss, as they both hold their heads. Lawton and
Moss attempt to climb out of their battered van. Loggo, Jimmy and
Chrissie run up towards the roadway, but they see another van parked up
there, with two men waiting for them. The fraud men chase them back
towards the bridewell. They shout to Snowy.*

LOGGO/CHRISSIE. Sniffers, Snowy! Sniffers!

*Snowy appears at the window. Malloy arrives and tells them to climb
in the car.*

32. Exterior. Window.

Snowy is at the window. He looks out.

32a. Interior. Window.

Malloy arrives in his car. He screams out.

MALLOY. Get in. Get in.

Jimmy and Loggo and Chrissie approach him. They have no option.

32b. Exterior. Window.

*Snowy looks out of the window as he grabs the rope. He sees a couple of
the fraud section men holding the other end. Snowy turns wildly away
from the rope and the window. He runs out of the room and into the
corridor, but turns back, grabs his trowel, and then runs out again.*

33. Exterior. Malloy's site. Day.

*The Mercedes screams round the corner of the bridewell. Moss is
watching the car. It skids round the corner then continues.*

34.   Exterior. Roof outside Snowy's room. Day.

Malloy and the others are bounding down the road beneath where Snowy has his rope. As they come towards the window and the rope we see one more van swinging onto the site blocking the way. Snowy comes out of the door on to the roof and runs to the railings. He looks down. Malloy screams the Mercedes into reverse back towards the men now running towards him. Snowy is hurtling across the flat roof between the room he has plastered and the corridor where he has his second rope. As he runs into the building two fraud men run across the adjacent rooftop and climb over the railings.

35.   Interior. Corridor and stairs to window. Day.

Snowy is banging into the corridor. He looks behind himself as he reaches his rope and sees two fraud men entering the corridor. He looks down the stairs where he sees Lawton coming up towards him. Snowy grabs hold of the rope, swings out of the window, and starts to go down the rope. (The following action is seen in slow motion.) Snowy is still in vision as the banister gives way. The window frame comes apart and he falls.

36.   Exterior. Malloy's site. Day.

Snowy is falling. Malloy's car is now going forward, and Snowy's body drops right in front of it. The car skids to a halt and the four men inside jump out and go to the front of the car. Loggo takes one look and backs away fast and leans on a wall. The fraud men watch from their top window. Jimmy turns away. We see the fraud men approach in the green van.

JIMMY. Here they come.

CHRISSIE. Yeah, well, get goin'. *(He shoves Jimmy.)* Well go on – y' don't know him – an' anyway, what can y'do? He's dead.

Jimmy turns and races down the road towards the car park, followed by a fraud man. Malloy turns to Chrissie.

MALLOY. *(Leaning on the Mercedes.)* Look, tell them I just started you all, that I asked for your P45's, and that you were bringing them in tomorrow. Please. This could ruin me. Please listen to me. I'll give you a job, I will, *I'll make it worth your while.*

> *Moss has walked up behind them. Chrissie grabs Malloy by the lapels and pushes him. He falls to the ground by the car. Chrissie bends down by Snowy's body and looks at his blood ebbing away into the dirt. Moss starts reading the standard caution to Malloy.*

MOSS. By the powers invested in me as an officer of the Department of Employment, I am obliged to inform you that I am empowered to apprehend you from unlawfully employing certain persons who are claiming full unemployment benefit. Do you wish to say anything? You are not obliged to say anything, but if you do what you say will be taken down and may be used in evidence.

37.   Exterior. Malloy's site. Day.

Jimmy Johnson is running away through the building site, hotly pursued by a fraud man. Jimmy Johnson runs into the entrance to the Royal Hospital and picks up a bunch of flowers to hide his face behind. The action freezes as the sound of an ambulance siren is heard.

Moonlighter

DIXIE DEAN   Tom Georgeson
FREDA DEAN   Eileen O'Brien
KEVIN DEAN   Gary Bleasdale

At the DOE
ASSISTANT MANAGER   David Fleeshman
DIXIE'S CLERK   Gilly Coman
JACKIE MILLS   Cheryl Leigh

At the Docks
HAICH   Tony Haygarth
SCOTTY   Paul Barber
MARLEY   Martin Wyldeck
THIRD DOCKER   Jimmy Coleman
FOURTH DOCKER   Alan Wright

THE LAUGHING CAVALIER   Syd Newman
MALLOY   Shay Gorman
MARIE   Diane Baker
DANNY DEAN   Karl Lornie
JANET DEAN   Nicola Hollinshead
STEPHEN DEAN   Stephen Moss
CHRISSIE TODD   Michael Angelis
LOGGO LOGMOND   Alan Igbon
GEORGE MALONE   Peter Kerrigan
YOSSER HUGHES   Bernard Hill

1. **Exterior. Department of Employment building. Day.**

The opening shot establishes the Department of Employment building.

2. **Interior. Department of Employment building. Day.**

Dixie is asleep on a bench. He wakes. Someone arrives and sits down behind the grille. She is a counter-clerk, and has Dixie's claim in her hand.

CLERK. *(Calling out.)* Mr Dean. Mr Dean.

DIXIE. *(Looking round as he gets up.)* About time too.

CLERK. Pardon?

DIXIE. I've been waiting here f'forty minutes. If I'd known I would've brought a packed lunch.

CLERK. Well, the quicker we get this over with, the quicker you can go.

The clerk looks down at the claim. Then at Dixie again.

CLERK. You're not in a hurry to go anywhere are you?

DIXIE. Nah, I don't have to be back at work for ages yet. *(He smiles.)*

CLERK. *(Easily.)* I take it that was meant to be a joke?

DIXIE. Yeah, a sick one.

CLERK. Right . . . Name?

DIXIE. Thomas Ralph Dean.

CLERK. Age?

DIXIE. Forty-four.

CLERK. Date of birth?

DIXIE. Twenty-third of the third, nineteen thirty-eight.

CLERK. Where do you reside?

DIXIE. Forty-seven Maryvale, the Hilltree Estate.

CLERK. How long have you resided there?

DIXIE. Fourteen years.

CLERK. Are you resident at any other address?

DIXIE. The Penthouse Suite at the Holiday Inn.

CLERK. Are you resident at any other address?

DIXIE. No.

CLERK. Have you done any work since your last signing on?

DIXIE. No.

CLERK. Is your wife employed in any capacity?

DIXIE. No.

CLERK. Are any other members of your family employed in any capacity?

DIXIE. No.

CLERK. Do you intend to start work before your next signature?

DIXIE. No.

CLERK. Are you sure that you are not employed in any capacity?

DIXIE. Yes.

CLERK. Thank you, Mr Dean.

DIXIE. It's been a privilege and an honour.

He goes.

3.   Interior. Public lavatory cubicle. Night.

We see Dixie during the following night's work. He is a security guard for 'Southgate Security' on the docks. However we see him dressed in a normal, everyday winter manner until the end of the scene. He is sitting in a cubicle in a public toilet, on the toilet seat but with his trousers still on. He is nervous, smoking and looking at his watch as he waits. After a few seconds we hear someone enter the next toilet. Dixie looks at the wall between them. The toilet paper that has been thrust into a hole in the wooden dividing wall is being pushed into Dixie's side of the toilet. Dixie looks towards the small whittled spy hole. A small roll of five pound notes is slid through and falls to the floor. More toilet paper is thrust into the hole. We hear the other man going out of the toilet and off. Dixie looks again at the hole before picking up the money. When he unfolds the money, he doesn't seem at all happy. Dixie comes out of the toilet and takes his hat out of his mac pocket. He puts it on. In the mirror we see it is a security guard's hat.

4. Exterior. Public lavatory in docks. Night.

Dixie comes out of the toilet. It is early evening, going or just gone dark. The toilets are on the edge of the docks. A small cargo vessel is in the background about forty yards away, but otherwise the area is deserted. Dixie makes his way towards the vessel. As he approaches it, we see a Ford Cortina approach from the opposite direction, picking up speed as it goes. The driver puts his headlights on full beam, deliberately catching Dixie in their glare. He backs away, but the car reaches him and stops. Dixie approaches it. The car has 'Southgate Security' signwritten on it. The driver winds down the window and looks out at Dixie. We see the driver. He is Marley, the security man in charge of that area of the docks for Southgate Security. He is near retirement age, big, heavy-set, a former policeman. He is in full security uniform and still has the demeanour of a policeman. Everyone is suspect.

MARLEY. You're early.

DIXIE. *(He leans in.)* Er. Yeah. *(Defensively.)* Well. The same bus was late last night. Y'can't tell these days.

MARLEY. That's true enough.

There is an awkward pause as Dixie doesn't quite know what to do. He hesitates about going.

I expect you want your money?

DIXIE. Wouldn't go amiss.

MARLEY. Come and sit inside the car.

Dixie does so. Marley pulls a plain white envelope out of his pocket. Dixie takes it.

DIXIE. Oh, ta.

He puts it in the same inside top pocket as the other money, struggling slightly as he puts it in. He then uses his other hand to move the five pound notes aside. He glances up at Marley, who watches and notices without expression, and waits till Dixie has finished.

MARLEY. Aren't you goin' to count it?

DIXIE. No. It's alright. I trust y'.

MARLEY. Some security guard you must be then.

DIXIE. No, well, I mean . . . Oh, well, alright then.

Dixie goes gingerly to take the envelope out of his pocket, but Marley waves his hand, indicating Dixie not to bother. Marley drives to the gangway.

MARLEY. Should sail the day after tomorrow. So they say.

DIXIE. What happens then?

MARLEY. There'll be others. The port isn't quite dead yet. Despite the efforts of all concerned.

DIXIE. I mean, y'know . . .

MARLEY. Expect the firm'll keep you busy for the next few weeks, till the end of the contract. And then it's 'Goodnight Vienna'.

He stops his car, turns the engine off and gets out. Dixie gets out too.

DIXIE. What d'you mean?

MARLEY. *(Lighting a cheroot.)* Haven't you heard?

DIXIE. No. *(He shakes his head.)*

MARLEY. We've lost the security contract with the shippin' line. The fourth in eighteen months and the last one on these docks.

DIXIE. You're joking. Why's that?

MARLEY. Could it be because we're not security guards, walking around sayin', 'It's all right, I trust y''?

DIXIE. Hey now. Hang on. I mean, I've only been here a week.

MARLEY. *(Ignoring him.)* Who cares? Nobody else seems to these days, why the soddin' hell should I? *(He sighs.)* At least I've still got my police pension.

DIXIE. Are you going too?

MARLEY. They've told me already. Anyway you're no longer early and the Laughing Cavalier's up there waiting for y'. Have fun and y'never know y'might even find the dockers turning up for a game of cards later. Got to do somethin' to pass the time.

Marley gets into his car and drives off as Dixie goes up the gangway and along the deck.

5. Interior. Cargo ship. Night.

Dixie is 'between decks' in the hold of the boat. He is approaching another 'security guard' with the same lack of uniform, who is sitting on some sacks and a crate, facing the cargo in the hold, which is over one-third full. The guard has a limp and a large scar across the side of his face. Singing 'Nobody's Child'. Dixie walks towards him.

DIXIE. Alright. *(No answer.)* Y'can go now.

THE LAUGHING CAVALIER. I was goin' to.

The Cavalier stands up. Picks up his duffle bag.

DIXIE. That's what I like about this job – the comradeship.

His remark appears to have no effect, as The Laughing Cavalier walks a couple of paces away. But then he turns back.

THE LAUGHING CAVALIER. Y'haven't been here very long, have y'?

DIXIE. Nah, it just seems like a lifetime.

THE LAUGHING CAVALIER. Y'll soon learn – y' don't have

friends in this job. The only friends y' likely to have are those
that want favours. And they're no kind of friends at all.

*He walks away through the hatchway without waiting for a reply. As
he goes, two dockers saunter towards him wearing donkey jackets, jeans
and carpet slippers or plimsolls. Both are carrying dockers' hooks.
They pass The Laughing Cavalier.*

SCOTTY. There he goes, the ship's rat.

HAICH. Now leave him alone, Scotty. Show some respect for the
dead.

*Dixie sits on a crate. The two dockers approach Dixie facing the
hold. They sit at either side of him. They too look down.*

HAICH. Alright, it's Dixie isn't it? I'm Haich. *(Dixie nods.)* On all
night again are you? *(Dixie nods again.)* Nice night for it. *(No
answer. Pause.)* Be on again tomorrow night will y'? *(Dixie nods.)*
Be an even better night for it. *(He grins at Dixie, then looks across
at the second docker.)* Have a look for his tongue, Scotty, I think
he's lost it. *(Scotty lifts up a packing case and some sacks.)* Like it
here do y', Dixie? *(Dixie shrugs.)* Could be worse, eh.

DIXIE. Yeah. Suppose so.

HAICH. It's okay, Scotty. Y' can stop lookin'. He's found it
again. *(Back to Dixie.)* Nice boat, isn't it?

DIXIE. It's alright, as boats go.

HAICH. Oh, it's more than that. It's even more than nice. I'd
even go as far as to say it had personality . . . character.

SCOTTY. Charm even. *(He drifts away towards the hold.)*

HAICH. Oh aye, yeah. Charm as well. Especially charm.

*Three more dockers arrive, wearing plimsolls and carrying dockers'
hooks.*

HAICH. *(Getting up.)* Alright lads, I was just telling Dixie here,
it's a superb boat this.

The third and fourth dockers nod.

HAICH. Do you know why?

DIXIE. No.

HAICH. It hasn't got containers.

Haich moves to the edge of the hold. We see Scotty rooting about. Haich shouts down.

HAICH. Try over there by that Nigerian dried milk, Scotty.

Dixie hears Scotty rooting about in the hold. He gets up and joins the dockers at the edge of the hold.

DIXIE. What . . . what's y' mate up to down there?

They look down.

HAICH. Oh he's a strange lad is Scotty. He always thinks of things in terms of a football match. *(He leans forward and looks down.)* It's his philosophy in life. I expect he's tryin' t'break through the defence. Bit of a Kenny Dalglish is Scotty. Y've got t' keep y'eye on him all the time.

DIXIE. Look, y'do know what I'm supposed t' be doin' here, don't y'?

HAICH. Yeah, you're the goalkeeper.

SCOTTY. Here they are Haich. *(He starts to open the crate.)*

HAICH. And it looks as though y've just conceded a goal. *(He moves back.)*

SCOTTY. Right, what sizes d' y' want?

He starts to throw boots.

HAICH. Nines f'me, Scotty.

THIRD DOCKER. Got any elevens?

SCOTTY. Elevens coming up.

FOURTH DOCKER. Eights for me and two pair of sevens for me lads.

The dockers are still surrounding Dixie. There is something stylized, rehearsed about their movements. Dixie stares at them, then at the second docker, who throws one pair of boots up, soon followed by others.

SCOTTY. What about you, pal?

DIXIE. Who?

HAICH. *(Quietly.)* You.

DIXIE. What?

HAICH. What size d' you take? *(Pushing him.)* Put your foot there, put it alongside mine. . . . *(Putting his foot by Dixie's.)*

DIXIE. Now look, lads . . .

HAICH. Nines. Scotty. Get him nines. Take y'shoes off, Dixie – y' could do with a new pair.

DIXIE. Are you pullin' my pisser?

HAICH. Not unless y'keep it in y'shoe pal. Here y' are. Sit down.

DIXIE. No.

HAICH. Come 'head.

Haich is pushing Dixie back towards the crates. The others gather round.

DIXIE. *(Sitting.)* Ah no, you're not on.

HAICH. Why not?

Dixie holds the boots up.

DIXIE. I can't wear these.

HAICH. Y've got the wrong size, Scotty.

DIXIE. But I'm a security guard.

HAICH. We all have a cross to bear.

DIXIE. I'm here to stop you.

The third and fourth dockers lean over him holding their dockers' hooks close to Dixie's face and then Haich leans over him.

HAICH. . . . And are you gonna stop us?

DIXIE. . . . I don't want any trouble, y' know. This . . . isn't me real job.

HAICH. Course it's not. You're on the dole. Aren't y'?

Dixie nods.

DIXIE. Yeah.

HAICH. You're not alone, blue. There's only Marley and his Ford Cortina that's real down here, the rest of the crowd're the same as you. Don't worry about it.

The dockers all bend down to put their new boots on.

DIXIE. Look. I just don't want no trouble like, you know.

HAICH. Y' won't get any, go 'head.

Scotty arrives.

DIXIE. But won't nobody say nothing?

SCOTTY. Yeah, they'll go friggin' mad in South Africa.

HAICH. And by the time they arrive there, this boat'll've been to three other ports. *(He laughs.)* They'll be lucky to have any boots left.

The dockers are still putting their boots on.

SCOTTY. So there y' are.

HAICH. Safe and sound.

SCOTTY. So long as you don't tell anyone, now Dixie.

HAICH. 'Cos that wouldn't be very nice, would it?

SCOTTY. We wouldn't like you anymore.

HAICH. Just when we were gettin' to know y'.

SCOTTY. It'd be a crying shame.

HAICH. We'd be upset.

SCOTTY. As well as angry.

HAICH. But you'd be the one who was hurt.

Dixie looks at them.

SCOTTY. So there.

HAICH. See. Come on. Scotty, stand on me boots, will you, scuff 'em up a bit.

> *Haich and Scotty stand on each other's boots. The others follow suit. They start dancing and singing 'These boots were made for walking'. Dixie looks down at his own boots. Dockers sing: 'One of these days these boots are going to walk all over you.'*

6. Exterior. Docks. Day.

It is daylight, the following morning. Dixie is on his way home. He walks along the sea-wall.

7. Exterior. George's road. Day.

Funeral cars and wreaths are lined up outside George's house. There are also private cars and an ambulance with two ambulancemen standing nearby, smoking. Four or five people come out of the house and get into cars. Amongst them are Loggo and Chrissie. Chrissie is dressed formally in black. They stop and Loggo lights up a cigarette. Dixie approaches. All three are flat and uneasy throughout.

CHRISSIE. Alright Dixie.

LOGGO. Dix.

DIXIE. Snowy?

CHRISSIE. Yeah.

DIXIE. I heard.

CHRISSIE. You were nearly there. That was the mornin' I called for you and y'—

DIXIE. I know. *(He looks towards the Malones' front door.)* George?

CHRISSIE. Don't ask, Dix. *(A pause.)*

LOGGO. How're you keepin' anyway – long time no see.

He offers Dixie a cigarette but it is a waste of time.

DIXIE. Yeah, the last time was Middlesbrough, Loggo.
Remember?

*They look at each other. Loggo and Chrissie give Dixie the victory of
looking away.*

I'm doing alright, I'm gettin' by.

CHRISSIE. *(Looking down.)* Goin' for long walks?

DIXIE. Bus never came.

CHRISSIE. I hear it's nights. *(Dixie nods.)* Still signin' on?

DIXIE. No option.

CHRISSIE. Yeah, well. Be careful.

DIXIE. *(Looking away.)* In more ways than one.

*Loggo turns and sees Snowy's coffin being brought out by the funeral
attendants and family as Dixie finishes speaking. The ambulancemen
approach. Loggo stubs out his cigarette and stands aside. George comes
out of the house, supported lightly by two men of his age, his
brothers, perhaps. A small family group follows. George is near to but
not in tears. We almost hear him before we see him.*

GEORGE . I'm goin' in the car, I'm not goin' there in that, tell
them I'm goin' in the car, will y'.

*The two men release their grip on him, and he walks slowly but
firmly towards the first car as the coffin is slid into the hearse. The
other mourners get in the cars. Loggo, Chrissie and Dixie are looking
down.*

LOGGO. I'm off. I can't stand requiems and cemeteries.

*Loggo walks quickly away, head down, the way Dixie has come.
Chrissie and Dixie walk to funeral car.*

CHRISSIE. See y', Dix.

Dixie looks up.

Hey if you're around our way . . . well, you know, y'know where I live.

DIXIE. *(Walking off.)* What d' you want me to do - 'make friends'?

Dixie turns and walks off. Chrissie hesitates a second and then gets into one of the cars. The doors on the funeral cars close, and the back door of the hearse is slammed shut.

8. Interior. Dixie's hall. Day.

Two letters are lying on the floor by the door in Dixie's hall. One of them is in a brown government envelope. We hear Dixie open the front door and see his new boots. He sees the letters, picks them up and moves towards the living room.

9. Interior. Dixie's living room. Day.

Dixie's living room is part of a three up and two down new council house. It is very tidy. Dixie's middle son, Danny, aged nearly sixteen, is lying on the sofa reading a magazine and listening to music.

9a. Interior. Hall.

Dixie walks through the hall.

9b. Interior. Living room.

Danny, in a pyjama top, jeans and bare feet, is eating toast. When he hears his dad coming, he shoves the plate of toast under a cushion. He tries to look sick and holds his stomach. Dixie enters and is about to open the letters when he sees Danny who groans.

DIXIE. What are you doin' here, Danny?

DANNY. I'm not . . .

DIXIE. Get dressed an' get to school, go on.

DANNY. But I've had these . . . *(He clutches his stomach.)*

DIXIE. Where's y' mother?

DANNY. She's . . . *(He points towards the back kitchen wall.)*

DIXIE. Are Kevin an' Janet here?

DANNY. They're still in . . . *(He points upstairs.)*

DIXIE. Is Stephen at home as well?

DANNY. He's . . . *(He points through the front windows of the house.)*

Dixie goes to the door and shouts.

DIXIE. Freda, Freda!

9c. Interior. Kitchen.

Freda looks out of the kitchen. She is an attractive vague redhead in her early forties. She does her very best.

9d. Interior. Living Room.

Dixie turns back to Danny.

DIXIE. How many times have I told you about trying it on with y' mother?

DANNY. But I've got a sore stomach, dad, honest.

DIXIE. Y'll have a sore arse if you're not off it an' up those stairs. Now go on, git!

Danny gets up quickly, half expecting a clout as he goes past Dixie. He gets one. They go out towards Freda in the hall.

10. Interior. Hall. At bottom of stairs.

DIXIE. Hey!

DANNY. What now? *(He stops.)*

DIXIE. What chances have y' got of leavin' school with any qualifications if y' never there in the first place?

DANNY. *(With contempt.)* Qualifications . . .

DIXIE. What's wrong with qualifications?

DANNY. Y' need nuclear physics t'be a binman these days, dad.

Danny goes up the stairs. Dixie points his finger as if to argue, then stops. He looks at the letters again as he goes into the hallway, and then to the kitchen door. Dixie kisses Freda.

DIXIE. I'm going to bed, girl. That seems t'be the fashion in this house.

Dixie opens the electricity bill, then starts to open the other letter as Freda follows him upstairs.

FREDA. They don't mean any harm, Tommy, they just don't listen to me . . .
DIXIE. Oh, for Christ's sake! *What are they doin'?*

FREDA. It's cheek mainly, an' stayin' in bed, but . . .

At the top of the stairs Dixie hands the letter to Freda. Janet comes out of the bathroom. ('Morning dad, mum'.) She goes between them and enters her room. Dixie opens the door. She closes it on him.

11. Interior. Dixie's landing and boys' bedroom. Day.

Freda has just realized that Dixie is referring to the letter. They have reached the landing facing the boy's bedroom. Danny and young Stephen share bunk beds, Kevin has a bed of his own. Dixie leans on the top banisters and flicks the letter at Freda. Then he looks into the boys' room and sees Danny putting his school uniform onto his bed. He also sees Kevin flat out asleep.

DIXIE. Look at him, just look at him – soddin' Sleepin' Beauty . . .

Dixie goes into the bedroom.

FREDA. But what does it mean?

DIXIE. It means I'm not goin' to bed.

Dixie goes to the bathroom. Freda follows.

FREDA. I thought you went there yesterday though.

DIXIE. Too true I did.

He is washing his face.

FREDA. What do they want you for again?

DIXIE. Maybe they've found me a job?

He goes into their bedroom to change.

FREDA. *(Sitting down.)* That'd be nice.

12.   Interior. Department of Employment building. Day.

Dixie is back at his previous position at the counter of the DOE. He is looking at the clerk from his previous test check.

DIXIE. What do you mean, you don't know nothin' about it – what's this, then? *(He puts the paper up at the grille; she jumps.)* A chain letter? Look at it – look! *(He pushes it under.)*

CLERK. But I've already looked, Mr Dean, and I've . . .

DIXIE. Get me someone worth talkin' to – come on, come on.

CLERK. But my . . .

DIXIE. *Get someone.*

CLERK. I'm trying to tell you, this letter wasn't sent by my department.

DIXIE. *Well who sent it then?*

The Assistant Manager of the Fraud Section appears as if he had been waiting for this cue. He is in his mid-thirties. He wears a leather jacket and lots of contempt. He has Dixie's claim in his hand.

ASSISTANT. Mr Dean?

Dixie nods.

DIXIE. Yes.

ASSISTANT. Thought it might be. We sent the letter, Mr Dean.

He walks out from behind the grille. Dixie joins him.

DIXIE. And who are you when you're out?

ASSISTANT. The Employment Section.

He motions to Dixie to go into the interview room. They do and he closes door. The Assistant Manager goes through and summons the clerk.

ASSISTANT. Jean - would you mind?

She gets up and joins him in the interview room.

ASSISTANT. Thank you.

She sits. Dixie sits reluctantly.

DIXIE. Yeah alright, but before we start, this is the second day runnin', an' the third time in a month I've been called in – now what's the score?

ASSISTANT. Routine. Merely administrative routine.

Walks round Dixie.

DIXIE. I can use big words as well, y'know. (*He leans forward with confidence and enunciates carefully.*) 'Elastoplast'.

The Assistant Manager doesn't flicker. Dixie leans back sourly. The Assistant Manager sits.

CLERK. Name?

DIXIE. Y'already know it. Y've used it y'self.

CLERK. Name?

DIXIE. And so did he.

CLERK. Name?

DIXIE. Are y' sure this isn't a trick question?

As the clerk goes to ask his name again, Dixie joins in, then answers the question. He continues in the same manner.

CLERK. Name?

DIXIE. Thomas Ralph Dean.

CLERK & DIXIE. Age?

DIXIE. Forty-four.

CLERK & DIXIE. Date of birth?

DIXIE. Twenty-third of the third, nineteen thirty-eight.

CLERK & DIXIE. Where do you reside?

DIXIE. Forty-seven Maryvale Street, the Hilltree Estate.

CLERK & DIXIE. How long have you resided there?

DIXIE. Fourteen years.

The clerk changes the order of the questions as she and Dixie speak together.

CLERK. Are you employed in any capacity?

DIXIE. Are you resident at – ah, you changed the order of the questions! That's not fair!

CLERK. Mr Dean—

DIXIE. *(He points.)* You're a cheat.

ASSISTANT. Mr Dean, you must realize that nothing can be gained from treating our enquiries in this manner. It quite obviously helps neither you nor I, and furthermore, you're hardly original in your approach. Quite frankly, it has been some years now since I have found even the slightest glimmer of amusement in antics of this nature. *(He nods at the clerk to carry on.)*

CLERK. Are you employed in any capacity?

DIXIE. *(To Assistant.)* Do you practice makin' speeches?

CLERK. *Are you employed in any capacity?*

DIXIE. Nah, I never have the time, do I. I'm always too busy comin' here. It costs 32 pence on the bus, too.

ASSISTANT. In most cases these test checks are picked out at random, Mr Dean, if that's any help to you.

DIXIE. The bus fare'd be more help.

Then the clerk continues and Dixie looks away.

CLERK. Have you done—

CLERK & DIXIE. —any work since you last signed?

DIXIE. No.

CLERK. Is your wife—

CLERK & DIXIE. —employed in any capacity?

DIXIE. No. Are any other members of your family employed in any capacity? No. Do you keep budgerigars in the bathroom? No.

ASSISTANT. Are you sure about the last question you were asked, Mr Dean.

DIXIE. Yeah, they'd shit all over the place wouldn't they? *(But he's not quite so confident.)* Which one?

ASSISTANT. The one with regard to your wife.

DIXIE. Yeah.

ASSISTANT. Not being employed in any capacity.

DIXIE. That's what I said, wasn't it.

ASSISTANT. Nothing at all?

DIXIE. *No.*

ASSISTANT. Not even a couple of hours a day, cleaning. Something like that. Helping her friends run a little . . . business?

DIXIE. I said no before, didn't I.

ASSISTANT. Well. Perhaps she hasn't told you. Women can be forgetful, you know.

DIXIE. *Look, what the hell is this?*

ASSISTANT. I've finished now, Mr Dean. Thank you, You can go.

The counter-clerk looks at the Assistant Manager, then at her papers. Dixie gets up and goes without comment. The Assistant makes a brief note in Dixie's claim as he talks. The clerk packs up and gets up to go.

ASSISTANT. So he wants to play funny buggers, does he . . . Do me a favour, would you – go over to my section and find out who we've got floating this afternoon. See who finds it funny then . . .

CLERK. If you don't mind me asking, there's nothing about his wife in there.

ASSISTANT. *(As he finishes writing.)* That's correct.

CLERK. How did you know?

ASSISTANT. I didn't. *(He grins and puts the claim away in his briefcase, then takes out another one as he talks.)* We . . . er . . . got some information the day before yesterday, from someone who's proved to be reliable in the past, indicating that half his road are claiming for their wives while their wives are working. So I've got everyone in that road who's signing on coming in this afternoon. Put the fear of God into them if nothing else. *(Looks down at the next claim.)* Stephen Jefferies please . . .

She goes out.

13. Interior. Dixie's living room. Day.

Dixie's daughter, Janet, is in the room with her dressing gown on, dancing. Dixie and Freda enter, Dixie first.

DIXIE. He knew. I'm telling you, he knew.

He stubs out his cigarette.

FREDA. But who told him?

DIXIE. I didn't like to ask.

FREDA. Oh.

DIXIE. Someone's blown you up, Freda.

He takes his coat off.

FREDA. But who'd do a thing like that?

DIXIE. More people than y' realize. Come on, Janet, will y'.

Freda takes Dixie's coat out.

JANET. What?

DIXIE. The time!

He goes.

13a. Interior. Kitchen.

Dixie joins Freda in the kitchen.

FREDA. Does that mean I'll have to stop?

She makes the coffee.

DIXIE. What do you think?

FREDA. It's only a pound an hour, three afternoons a week.

DIXIE. Y'may as well be sellin' state secrets to the Russians, it's all the same t'them.

FREDA. You won't be able to go to the docks, Tommy, if they're checkin' up.

DIXIE. I've got to go tonight.

He goes to the table.

FREDA. Surely you could give it a miss for one night.

DIXIE. I can't.

He sits down. Freda joins him.

FREDA. Don't get upset, Tommy, y'know it—

DIXIE. Janet!

Dixie jumps up.

13b. Interior. Living room.

Dixie storms into the living room and pushes Janet onto the sofa.

DIXIE. It's gone twelve o'clock.

JANET. So?

Dixie turns the record off.

DIXIE. So get upstairs and get some clothes on!

JANET. *(She gets up.)* But what for?

DIXIE. Don't 'what for' me, girl, just get up there and do it.

She goes towards the hall. He follows.

13c. Interior. Hall.

JANET. There's no need t'take it out on me.

Janet begins to go up the stairs with Dixie following as he speaks to Freda.

DIXIE. What did she say?

FREDA. *(Lying.)* I never heard her.

DIXIE. *(To Janet.)* What did you say then?

Janet leans over from the landing.

JANET. Nothin'. An' anyway our Kevin's still in bed.

Dixie looks at Freda.

FREDA. I have shouted him.

DIXIE. Some job he'll get, lyin' in bed all day.

Dixie runs up the stairs. Freda waits at the bottom.

FREDA. Er no, don't go up, Tommy, I'll get him now.

Dixie rounds the top of the stairs, goes out of view and shouts.

DIXIE. Kevin!

14. Interior. The boys' bedroom. Day.

Kevin is fast asleep in his single bed. We hear Dixie bouncing up the stairs. The door opens. Dixie goes to the side of the bed.

DIXIE. Kevin. Come on, get up.

Kevin mumbles as he is wakened.

DIXIE. D'you know what time it is?

KEVIN. Er . . . No. *(He yawns.)*

DIXIE. It's quarter past twelve.

KEVIN. Is that all?

DIXIE. I want you to get up.

KEVIN. It's too early, Dad. Anyway, what is there to get up for?

Dixie grabs the duvet and hurls it away from the bed.

DIXIE. Get up!

KEVIN. What d'you do that for?

DIXIE. Because y' a bloody disgrace, Kevin. You're not even tryin' any more.

KEVIN. Leave off, will y', just leave off.

DIXIE. Get y' clothes on an' get out an' look f' work.

KEVIN. There is none.

They are both shouting.

DIXIE. There is none when y' lyin' in bed.

KEVIN. An' there's none when I'm walkin' up an' down the industrial estate neither! You know that – you've been there with me as well. I've been left school two-and-a-half years. I've been out of work for two of them, and I've never so much as had a bastard interview. *(Kevin punches his bed.)* So don't give me no crap about lyin' in bed.

Kevin gets off the bed, grabs the duvet, lies down and covers himself. Dixie seems set to explode further, but he can't find the words. He tries for a second or two and then goes out. We hold for a second or two, as Dixie slams the door shut and then Danny begins to crawl out from under the bottom bunk where he has been hiding. He is still in his pyjama top and jeans. The phone begins to ring downstairs.

15. Interior. Dixie's hall. Day.

There is a pay-phone to one side of the bottom of the stairs. It is ringing. Dixie is at the bottom of the stairs. He picks the phone up.

DIXIE. Yeah?

VOICE. *(Pleasant, insidious.)* Dixie Dean?

DIXIE. That's right.

VOICE. Now you don't know me, but you got a little bonus off a friend of mine last night, a fifty pound bonus just for starters, and all I'm doing, Dixie, is giving you a little reminder that if you want the rest of the bonus and you want to keep your features you'll be a good little boy tonight.

The phone goes dead immediately. Dixie looks at the receiver, again at a loss for words.

16. Interior. Dixie's hall.

Freda has her coat in her hands. As Dixie returns, we see her putting it on.

FREDA. Who was that?

DIXIE. Oh, er, no one, nothin'. *(He looks at her.)* What are you doin'?

FREDA. I've got to tell the other girls, I can't just leave them.

DIXIE. Y' jokin' aren't y'?

FREDA. They'll all be waitin' for me.

DIXIE. An' that's just what they want.

FREDA. Oh. Er . . . Who?

DIXIE. You go see other girls, right? Bad man with binoculars
see you, right? Bad man follows you, sees you meet other girls in
mo-mo car – right?

Freda starts to undo her coat.

FREDA. Alright Tommy.

DIXIE. Bad man follows nice girls, sees nice girls puttin' leaflets
through letter boxes for pound notes, no questions asked, make
bad man with binoculars happy, bad man rides into town, forms
posse, nice girls get captured.

*Dixie turns into the lounge. Freda speaks with dignity as she takes
her coat off.*

FREDA. I'm not completely soft, y'know. You don't have to talk
to me like that. Before you went on the docks, we needed the
money I got with the girls, it was the only money we had
coming in.

DIXIE. I know, I know.

FREDA. Your Giro doesn't go far, Tommy. Not with—

Dixie screams his reply.

DIXIE. I know!

He goes into the lounge. Freda follows.

17.   Interior. Lounge.

*Dixie goes to the window, looks out, and pauses. Dixie turns away from
the lace curtains, to the easy chair. Freda comes to the door.*

FREDA. . . . D' y' want some dinner?

DIXIE. Nah, I've got to get some sleep. *(He sits down.)* And
listen, if anyone comes sniffin' around asking questions, wantin'
to come in, I don't care who they say they are, you don't tell
them nothin', an' you don't let them in.

Dixie takes his new boots off. Freda walks in, sits down.

FREDA. Surely they wouldn't come here? *(Dixie looks at her sadly.)* They're not allowed t'come in are they, an' just . . .

DIXIE. Y' don't know much about the ways of the world, do y'?

FREDA. But that's terrible. What am I going to say?

DIXIE. *(Picking up his boots.)* You don't say nothing. You don't even open the door.

FREDA. Where d'y' get the boots?

DIXIE. *(He puts them down.)* They fell off a boat.

He puts his hand into his jacket pocket, takes out the envelope containing his wages. He throws the envelope in her lap. Then pulls out the other money, peels off three five-pound notes and hands her the rest. She looks at the roll of fivers, bewildered.

FREDA. Who give y' all this?

DIXIE. A man in a toilet.

Dixie picks the boots up and stands.

FREDA. Are you feelin' alright, Tommy.

DIXIE. Don't worry.

He goes out and she follows him into the hall.

17a. Interior. Hall.

FREDA. You're not in any trouble, are y'?

DIXIE. You ask more questions than the dole, you do.

FREDA. But Tommy . . .

DIXIE. Get y'self somethin'. Somethin' for y'self.

He starts to go up the stairs. Freda stares at the envelope and the money. She is becoming scared. She goes into the kitchen.

17b. Interior. Kitchen.

Freda is in the kitchen. Dixie and Danny are out of view but we hear them.

DIXIE. Hey Danny, what the friggin' hell do you think you're doing?

DANNY. Me mam said I could . . . *(There is a loud smack.)* Ow! Array, dad.

18. Interior. Dixie's kitchen.

Freda comes to the window and looks out. There is a red Ford Escort parked a few yards away but all we can see, and only vaguely, are a blonde woman and a man. Freda sees the car and hides the money in a cake tin. An old battered Mini arrives with three women inside of the same age and class as Freda. Freda reaches for the blind as one of them gets out and comes up the path to knock on the door. Freda, looking worried, closes the blind and waits. The woman then looks through the front window but Freda closes a second blind. The woman goes back to the door, and starts knocking.

19. Interior. Dixie's hallway. Day.

Freda has crept from the kitchen and crawled round to the front door.
We see Freda up against the door. She has lifted the letterbox lid – two-thirds of the way up the door – and is talking through it. She doesn't see any comedy in the situation at all. All we can see of the other woman, Marie, are her eyes, and when she talks, her mouth.

FREDA. Stop knockin' will y'.

MARIE. But we've been waitin' ages for y'.

FREDA. I can't come out, Marie.

MARIE. Is one of the kids ill?

FREDA. No, it's them – they're after me.

MARIE. They're what?

FREDA. They're after me.

MARIE. Who are?

FREDA. The whatsits – the dole.

MARIE. Since when?

FREDA. They had Tommy in this mornin', questionin' him about me. They know what's goin' on.

MARIE. *(After a pause.)* What is going on?

FREDA. The job – the leaflet thingies.

MARIE. Ah, we've been doin' it for years, Freda. They'd have caught us by now. Come on, get y' coat on.

FREDA. I can't. It's not safe, I might be followed.

MARIE. We're givin' away threepence off cornflakes, not robbin' banks, now are y' comin' or what?

FREDA. I daren't. Y'd better go, Marie, they could be watchin' us right now.

MARIE. Don't worry, they'll just think I'm kissin' y' door.

FREDA. *(She turns in.)* Go 'way. Please go away.

MARIE. . . . Bloody hell, Freda.

Marie goes. Freda sits facing out.

20. Exterior. Dixie's house. Day.

Marie moves her lips away from the letterbox. Then she walks away towards the gate as a young window cleaner comes up the path with a bucket and ladder.

MARIE. Y' wastin' y' time there, lad.

He looks at Marie and then carries on. He rings the bell to ask for some water. As he does so, the letterbox lifts up.

FREDA. Go next door. *(He stares at the letterbox.)* Go on, if y'
want water, go next door. And if you're on the dole, be
careful, I'm being followed.

*The letterbox snaps shut. The window cleaner looks around himself,
shakes his head and moves quickly away. We see Marie and the
others in the car. Marie has obviously told the others. They are
shrieking with laughter as the car goes. We hold on the scene as the
Ford Escort begins to follow. Only the driver, the man, is now in the
car. The blonde woman, Jackie Mills, has got out of the car and is
crossing to Freda's front door.*

21. Interior. Dixie's hallway. Day.

*There is knocking on the door. Freda is at the door of the living room,
hidden from the hall.*

FREDA. Oh sweet Jesus . . . *(She moves towards the coatrack and
hides.)* What do y' want?

We hear a terribly cheerful, confident and cosmetic voice.

JACKIE MILLS. Hello Mrs Dean.

FREDA. Er . . . hello.

JACKIE MILLS. It is Mrs Dean, isn't it. *(Freda goes to open her
mouth.)* I'm Jackie Mills, your perfume party representative.

FREDA. Since when?

JACKIE MILLS. You've been recommended to us, Mrs Dean.

FREDA. It's news to me.

JACKIE MILLS. Nevertheless, if I could just have a few moments
of your time, to have the opportunity to show you the many
new and exciting perfumeries and cosmetics in our 1982 range,
which, if you would permit me to hold a party at your home,
you will be allowed to purchase at over thirty percent off retail
price, and also enable you to enter our free competition for a
weekend in Paris for two!

FREDA. No.

JACKIE MILLS. Please, Mrs Dean, if you could spare the time to see our superb catalogue of—

FREDA. Me husband's in bed, I don't want to disturb him.

JACKIE MILLS. Oh I am sorry, I didn't realize, is he on night work?

Freda is about to say 'yes', but manages to check herself.

FREDA. . . . he's . . . ill. He's ill in bed.

Thereupon the phone rings.

FREDA. There's the phone, I'll have to go. Goodbye. Thank you.

She goes to the phone.

JACKIE MILLS. Don't worry about me, Mrs Dean, I can wait a few moments.

Freda turns to the phone and picks it up.

FREDA. 2033.
We hear the man who spoke earlier to Dixie.

VOICE. Now would that be Mrs Dean?

FREDA. No, it's the Queen of friggin' Sheba. Now what d' y' want?

VOICE. *(As he laughs warmly.)* Your husband.

FREDA. He's in bed.

VOICE. Well, when he gets up, darlin', tell him the man with the bonus rang – tell him I was talkin' to you – and that depending on certain events, we might meet one day, you and I.

The phone goes dead. Freda is out of her depth. She puts down the phone, and then makes for the door.

FREDA. Now look here, I don't want no soddin' perfume, and I don't—

We hear Malloy's voice coming warmly through the door from a position out of Freda's sight. Then he moves into view.

MALLOY. Hullo Mrs Dean, it's me, Franky Malloy love . . .

22. Exterior. Dixie's house. Day.

We cut to outside the door as Malloy talks. Jackie Mills is still there.
She is a well-dressed attractive blonde in her late twenties, holding a
clipboard and carrying a shoulder bag. She does look like a perfume
representative. Malloy looks tired and slightly crumpled, despite the charm
and warmth of his voice.

MALLOY. Is Dixie there?

FREDA. He's in bed, he's ill.

MALLOY. It's nothin' serious is it?

FREDA. Yes, no, I don't know.

MALLOY. Not workin' then?

FREDA. No.

MALLOY. Look, can I come in for a minute, I feel a bit of a—

FREDA. No.

MALLOY. I'm offerin' Dixie some work and some ready—

FREDA. Ssssshhhhhhhhh!

MALLOY. What?

FREDA. *(Gabbling.)* I'm bein' investigated, Mr Malloy. It's not
safe to talk. I'm at risk, and you've been done yourself by the
dole, Tommy told me, so go away, just go away. I can't take
much more.

> *There is a pause as Malloy looks at the door, then glances at the*
> *girl.*

MALLOY. Yeah, all right. But when he gets up, ask him if he'd
be interested in a few weeks' work. Tell him I'll give him a ring
later, okay . . .

Malloy turns away. Jackie Mills speaks to Freda through the letterbox.

JACKIE MILLS. I'll be going now as well, Mrs Dean. I can see it's obviously not an appropriate time. I'll call again. Bye!

There is no answer, but then she hasn't waited for one. She catches up with Malloy as he reaches the garden gate. They walk towards Malloy's car.

JACKIE MILLS. Mr Malloy. My name's Jackie Mills, I'm a perfume representative for . . .

MALLOY. Sorry, I don't wear perfume and I don't like parties . . .

Jackie Mills laughs and then offers him her most alluring smile.

JACKIE MILLS. I hope you don't mind me asking, but I take it you're a married man?

Malloy stops, but then sets off again.

MALLOY. It shows, does it?

JACKIE MILLS. Not at all, but I wonder if your wife would like to hold a party in your house to display the many new and exciting perfumeries and cosmetics in our 1982 range.

Malloy is getting into his car.

MALLOY. *(With no edge and hardly any interest.)* Sorry, y' wastin' your time, love. My wife buys her make-up in bulk.

He drives off. Three or four schoolchildren aged about twelve approach from across the road. She watches as Malloy drives away. She looks between the children to see his registration number. She writes it on her clipboard.

23. Interior. Dixie's hall. Day.

Freda is lighting a cigarette. She is sitting on the floor with her back to the door. We hear another knock on the door.

FREDA. Frig off, whoever you are!

Outside is a confused eleven-year-old Stephen.

STEPHEN. It's only me, Mam.

She gets up and lets him in, picks up the ashtray and leaves.

24. Interior. Dixie's bedroom. Night.

It is dark inside Dixie and Freda's bedroom though there are hints of light from behind the curtains. Dixie is asleep. An alarm goes off, then stops. Dixie switches on the bedside lamp. He climbs out of bed in his underwear. There are a suitcase and a grip on top of a wardrobe, plus the usual double bed, dressing table, chest of drawers. Dixie slips his trousers on.

25. Interior. Dixie's landing. Night.

Dixie comes out onto the landing fastening his shirt. He begins to go downstairs, but stops and decides to go into the boys' bedroom next to his and Freda's room. The door is shut. Excellent 12-bar blues is being played on a guitar.

26. Interior. Boys' bedroom. Night.

The door is closed. The music stops as Dixie knocks. Dixie enters and stands by the door. Kevin is sitting on his bed, leaning back against the wall. In his sweat-shirt and underwear, guitar in hand. Danny is also in the room, reading a football magazine. He looks at Dixie as he enters and then buries his head in the magazine. Dixie stands in the doorway.

DIXIE. *(Flatly, finally.)* Quarter to six.

KEVIN. I'll get dressed in a minute.

Kevin starts playing again.

DIXIE. Why bother? Another few hours it'll be time for bed again.

KEVIN. I'm going out after.

DIXIE. Y' stay away from the police this time.

Kevin nods, Dixie looks at Danny who hides behind his magazine.

What are y' goin' to do?

Kevin stops playing.

KEVIN. Y' mean tonight?

DIXIE. No, I don't mean tonight.

KEVIN. . . . I'll make the rounds again tomorrow. There s a factory at the far end of the estate I haven't been to yet.

DIXIE. What about . . . What if you was to . . . D'you want a job?

Kevin looks at him coldly.

Yeah. All right. *(Dixie closes the door.)* What would happen if y' was to leave home? Would y' leave home.

Kevin nods slightly and Dixie notices this before looking away. He leans against the wall, then looks at Kevin again throughout the scene.

It's obvious none of us are helpin' each other. Fightin' never seems to lead anywhere 'cept to another fight. An' y' can still get a job out of town, y'know. Long contracts. The out-of-town-boys.

KEVIN. On the blackstuff?

DIXIE. Beggars can't be choosers.

KEVIN. Can lad and dogsbody.

DIXIE. I know it's not what y'want, Kevin. But what I'm doin' these days isn't what I want neither.

KEVIN. Y' don't have to tell me. I know that.

He smiles at his father. But Dixie doesn't notice the smile.

DIXIE. If I'd had any sense . . . if I'd . . . if I'd known what was goin' to happen, I wouldn't have done some of the things I have done. To you. I sort of . . . made a lot of mistakes with you, son.

*Kevin swallows. Dixie is looking down. Dixie opens the door which he
is nearly facing anyway. He rushes out and as he exits, the phone
goes downstairs. We stay in the room briefly. Danny lowers his
magazine and can hardly constrain his sniggers. He looks over at
Kevin and bursts out laughing. Kevin promptly throws a football at
him. It hits him hard and straight in the face.*

27.   Interior. Dixie's hall. Night.

*Freda and Stephen are in the kitchen. When the phone rings, she looks
out. Dixie is coming down the stairs. The phone is still ringing out.
Stephen is in the kitchen, spreading a chocolate spread butty. Freda is in
quiet bits. She sees Dixie and crosses out of the kitchen.*

FREDA. Oh Christ, Tommy, thank God you're up.

DIXIE. Answer the phone, will y'.

FREDA. I don't want to.

*She meets Dixie on the stairs. He looks at her as he reaches the
bottom of the stairs, then picks up the phone. He speaks cautiously.
She leans through the stairs.*

DIXIE. Yeah?

MALLOY. Dixie, hello there – it's Franky Malloy here.

DIXIE. Hallo, Malloy. What do you want?

FREDA. He's been to the house.

Dixie puts his hand over her mouth.

DIXIE. And whatever it is, count me out.

MALLOY. Dix, it's urgent. It's good money and it's sound.

DIXIE. *(Without anger.)* Sound – after what's been happenin' to
you? Y've just been caught red-handed and Snowy Malone dead
an' all. How sound is that?

MALLOY. Believe me . . .

DIXIE. And they're sniffin' around here and all. There's no
chance – we may as well carry banners around town announcin'
the time and place.

MALLOY. But this one's handsome, the firm isn't in my name, nobody—

DIXIE. Yeah, yeah. Thanks for the offer – you've helped me out before – but I'm up to my eyes in shi— *(He looks at Freda.)* —difficulties already. Sorry.

He puts the phone down and crosses to the lounge. She runs after him into lounge.

FREDA. There's been other phone calls, Tommy.

28. Exterior. Docks. Night.

Dixie is running through the warehouse. As he goes, we see the ship's mate watching him. It is the same part of the docks we saw earlier and is night again. Marley's car is by the side of the gangway, empty, with its sidelights on. Dixie is running up the gangway and continues along the deck.

29. Interior. Cargo ship. Deck. Night.

Marley, who is waiting at the boat rail, lights a cheroot and looks at his watch. Dixie walks along the deck towards him.

MARLEY. Don't tell me, it was the buses.

Dixie shakes his head.

DIXIE. No, the chauffeur was late.

MARLEY. I'm sorry to hear that.

DIXIE. Yeah, an' the au-pair couldn't find me cap. *(He digs the security hat out of his pocket.)* Y' let the Laughin' Cavalier go? *(Marley nods.)*
Ta.

Marley seems very relaxed.

MARLEY. Keep an eye on the sods tonight, last night in port, that's when they all start their little tricks.

DIXIE. Right. You be around?

MARLEY. Here and there.

  (He misses a beat.)

Why?

DIXIE. Just wondered, y'know. I mean if they got up to somethin'.

MARLEY. There's nothin' worth robbin' on this boat apart from a few crates of salmon and the odd pair of boots.

  Dixie fights against looking at his feet. Marley appears not to notice.

Anyway, I thought I might slip back to yours, see what your au-pair's like. *(He clicks his teeth.)*

DIXIE. An y' wouldn't stand a chance, the butler's bagged off with her.

  They both grin. Marley walks away. Dixie hesitates. Marley is now walking down the gangway. Dixie runs along the deck towards him.

DIXIE. Mr Marley! Mr Marley!

  Dixie catches up with Marley.

DIXIE. If f'some reason, like, I should need y', where will y' be?

MARLEY. They're off-loading precious metals on pier number three. I'll be there all night, me an' the Dock Police, searchin' dockers' pockets for gold nuggets.

  Marley goes off down the gangway.

DIXIE. Right.

  Dixie watches him go. We watch Dixie. We see anxiety take over, and how nervous he really is. He turns and walks up the gangway.

30. Interior. Cargo ship. The hold. Night.

Dixie crosses from the right while the dockers cross from the left. They meet in the middle.

DIXIE. All right lads, I'm off now.

OTHERS. Eh?

DIXIE. I'm going now.

HAICH. *(With genial contempt.)* Say that again.

DIXIE. I . . . I've just told y' – I was told to disappear.

HAICH. Who've you been talkin' to – Paul Daniels?

SCOTTY. That's a name to conjure with.

  They laugh.

DIXIE. Look. All I know is that when you lot start doin' whatever it is y' doin'—

SCOTTY. We were thinkin' of havin' a party.

HAICH. An' you're definitely on the invitation list.

DIXIE. But I was told to . . . my message was to stay out of the way for an hour or so.

  The dockers circle in. Haich shakes his head.

HAICH. Oh no. No no no no no.

DIXIE. No?

HAICH. No.

SCOTTY. No.

HAICH. *(To Dixie.)* You're not goin' nowhere pal. *(Haich smiles.)*

  Dixie goes to move away. They put their hooks on the wire guardrails to surround him.

DIXIE. Hey now look, I don't want no part of this.

HAICH. Except the money.

DIXIE. I'm gettin' paid for not bein' here.

HAICH. But I've just told you we're invitin' y' to stay.

SCOTTY. To the party.

DIXIE. That wasn't part of the arrangement. I don't do things like this. I'm not a thief.

HAICH. Thief. Thief! Did someone say thief? *(He turns to Scotty.)* Are you a thief?

SCOTTY. Not me. Must be you lah. *Looking at the third docker.)*

DIXIE. It's not my style.

HAICH. It is now, pal.

DIXIE. All I want t'do is keep me nose clean, keep out of the way an' clear off home.

HAICH. Tough.

  Dixie is visibly upset.

DIXIE. Look, my tart's had threatenin' phone calls all bloody day long about this. Now that's not good for me is it?

HAICH. But y'see, you bein' here is a sort of . . . a safety valve,

DIXIE. Oh I know, it bloody does.

HAICH. But y'see, you bein' here is a sort of . . . a saftey valve, you see, because with this job, we don't know who's settin' it up, 'cos it's a mystery this one. It's clever but it's got not trademark. It's not the usual system an' the same bunch of rogues. There's a big question mark about it. And y' see, if we're bein' set up . . . if someone like that bastard Marley is lookin' to go out with a bang, or someone like you, Dix, is lookin' to collect a few medals, we've got to have some insurance.

SCOTTY. Some cover.

HAICH. Against accidents.

SCOTTY. A kind of limited liability. *(To the others.)* Good, hey? Limited liability! *(But no one laughs.)*

HAICH. And you're all of those, you are Dix. *(But when he talks again, his tone is brutal.)* An' listen to me, Mr Clean, if y' thinkin' of lookin' down y' nose at us, let me tell you, the worst robbers on these docks are the so-called security guards – nothin's sacred t' some of your kind.

Royal Mail, personal effects, medical supplies, missions of mercy to
starvin' countries. I've seen men wearin' caps an' badges rip into all
of them an' y'know why – 'cos the likes of you, y'shite. You're
nothing. Y' the dregs, dragged here off the dole. Now stand
there an' do what y' supposed to do – watch us work.

*They all file past Dixie. We stay with Dixie who doesn't move. We
see, before he puts his head down, that he is beginning to weep
silently.*

We see the following rapid scenes.

31. Interior. Ship's hold. Night.

*The ship's mate is walking along the edge of the hold. He looks in to
see. The dockers are working deep in the bottom of the hold, moving and
lifting away any cargo that is in the way of the bonded locker, where the
goods of any value are kept. It is a compartment of varying size, usually
custom-built to the side of the hold and behind steel doors.*

32. Interior. Ship – between decks. Night.

*We see the ship's mate climb down the ladder in his uniform. He arrives
between decks. He looks at Dixie, who has his head down. The ship's mate
begins to climb further down into the hold.*

33. Interior. Ship's hold. Night.

*The dockers are taking boxes out of the bonded locker. The steel doors to
the bonded locker open, and the mate and Haich walk out of the doorway
smiling. Haich looks skywards out of the hold.*

HAICH. There's a van outside loading up now but I just want a
word with my mate here. *(He walks across and shouts.)* All right up top.
Bring the hook across. *(Turns to Scotty.)* Go upstairs an' keep an eye
out, Scotty. Take the toe rag with y'.

As the hook moves across Haich looks towards Dixie. Scotty leaves followed by Dixie. The dockers start fixing the hook to the crate.

34. Exterior. Ship deck/dockside. Night.

A van is parked up alongside the ship. Two men are throwing cartons of cigarettes off the crane palette into the van. We hear Dixie and Scotty before we see them.

DIXIE. Surely a load like that's goin' t'be missed?

SCOTTY. Oh, it will. But not off this boat. *(We see Dixie and Scotty leaning over the side. Scotty turns to Dixie.)* The boat that should be carryin' that lot sailed thirty-six hours ago. Our friend the first mate's just been lookin' after them, keepin' them in a safe place. For a favour. And a price. Everyone's got a price, right, all men can be bought, and the incorruptible man has the highest price of all.

DIXIE. Shite.

SCOTTY. No, Swift.

Scotty crosses to the hold and looks down.

Oh, very crusty, the first mate's gettin' the whisky out. See, I told you we were havin' a party.

He goes. When the men finish loading the van it is driven away. Dixie stays where he is, watching the tail lights of the van disappear. Dixie turns and looks into the hold. There is indeed a party going on. We see the first mate passing whisky around to a congregation of dockers.

35. Interior. Public lavatory cubicle. Day.

Dixie is in the same cubicle of the toilets as before. We see his boots on the toilet floor. He is in his socks. We hear someone enter the toilet, go past Dixie's cubicle and enter the next one. Dixie looks at the hole in the wall. The toilet paper comes out, followed by three separate rolls of ten-

pound notes, and then more toilet paper is shoved into place. Dixie takes the money. Dixie waits as he hears the other man opening the toilet door. He waits further till the man goes past, then he stands up on the toilet. He looks over the top of the cubicle door to see Marley walking away from him towards the mirror where he adjusts his hat and walks out of the toilet. Dixie ducks down. Dixie turns away and closes his eyes momentarily. Then takes his security hat off and flicks it into the toilet bowl. He flushes the toilet.

36. Interior. Dixie's house/stairs/landing/bedroom. Day.

Dixie walks up the stairs and into the bedroom. It is dark when he enters the bedroom. He crosses to wardrobe. We see Freda's reflection in the mirror. She is in bed. She makes a startled noise as he moves the case. Then she switches the lamp on. He takes suitcase down.

FREDA. What . . .

Looks at the alarm clock.

You're early Tommy.

He unzips the grip and sits.

DIXIE. Yeah. Well, after I took part in the robbery of half a million cigarettes and got my share of the proceeds, there wasn't much else for me to do. So I decided to come home.

He lies back on the bed. Freda sits up.

FREDA. Don't you think it'd be a good idea to go and see the doctor love? Y've been sort of . . . (She looks at the suitcase.) Tommy! Where y'goin'?

DIXIE. Out me mind. I'll be back in a minute – get my side of the bed warmed up, go on.

He gets up and leaves the room. She moves over.

37. Interior. Boys' bedroom. Day.

We see the boys' bedroom. Danny and Stephen, in their bunk beds, hear

Dixie open the door. Dixie enters and goes to Kevin's bed. Kevin is fast asleep. Dixie puts the grip down flat on the floor by the side of Kevin's bed. He unzips it and throws two rolls of ten-pound notes in. He looks at Kevin for a second or two, puts the third roll in, then goes.

38.   Exterior. Dixie's back door. Day.

Freda sees Kevin off down the path and away. She is crying.

39.   Exterior. Approach road to M62. Day.

Kevin is standing by the approach road to the M62. He is trying to hitch a lift. The action freezes.

Shop Thy Neighbour

CHRISSIE TODD   Michael Angelis
ANGIE TODD   Julie Walters

At the DOE
MISS SUTCLIFFE   Jean Boht
ASSISTANT MANAGER   David Fleeshman
· DONALD MOSS   David Ross
LAWTON   David Neilson
JACKIE MILLS   Cheryl Leigh
YOSSER HUGHES   Bernard Hill
LOGGO LOGMOND   Alan Igbon
GEORGE MALONE   Peter Kerrigan
MALLOY.   Shay Gorman
MRS SUTCLIFFE   Daisy Bell
GAS MAN   Jimmy Wilde

The Children
CLARE TODD Suzanne Harrison
JUSTINE TODD Clare Kelly
JASON HUGHES Timothy Bleasdale
ANNE MARIE HUGHES Tamana Bleasdale
DUSTIN HUGHES Jamie Bleasdale

1. Exterior. Back yard. Chrissie's house. Day.

We see the backs of a row of terraced houses one of which is Chrissie's.
We finish up on Chrissie's back yard. Chrissie and Angie are out of view but we hear the following dialogue.

CHRISSIE. Oh yeah, yeah, yeah. As ever, as bloody ever. You know, forever and ever – the same soddin' things.

ANGIE. And you know why they're the same soddin' things – because you do nothing about them. They don't go away on their own Chrissie. They don't go away because you lie in bed and mope about the house.

CHRISSIE. Oh, be quiet and give your arse a rest.

ANGIE. That's your department.

CHRISSIE. I said shut up.

ANGIE. I won't.

CHRISSIE. Shut up.

ANGIE. I won't shut up. Why should I shut up? You started it.

CHRISSIE. Oh yeah. What did I do?

ANGIE. Nothin'. That's how you started it.

Chrissie comes out of the back door leading to the yard. He slams it shut. The back kitchen door opens again. Angie looks out. The geese squawk.

ANGIE. I used to slam doors when I was seven!

She can't help herself and actually slams the door to close it. Chrissie half smiles, opens the door and leans in.

CHRISSIE. You haven't changed much, have you?

He closes the door again. Again the door is open by Angie. Just a flash.

ANGIE. It was the draught.

She closes it again.

CHRISSIE. *(To the geese.)* You can shut up an' all.

Chrissie half sighs, half grins. He moves further into the yard and picks up a bag of food.

CHRISSIE. Here.

We see that his yard is full of animals. A pigeon loft, a chicken pen, a ferret's cage, a rabbit's cage and a goose pen. There is a tortoise in the corner. He feeds the lettuce to the rabbit, then glances at the ferret.

CHRISSIE. You can die.

Chrissie looks in the pigeon's cage, and feeds the rabbit. We see the ferret. Angie is at the window putting on her coat. She opens the door.

ANGIE. I'm taking the kids to school.

CHRISSIE. Yeah all right.

Angie points to the animals.

ANGIE. I'm glad to see they're having their breakfast.

CHRISSIE. *(Flatly.)* Don't start, Angie.

ANGIE. Y'can feed y' soddin animals . . .

Chrissie is feeding the geese. He holds up a bag of vegetables.

CHRISSIE. I robbed these from the bins at the back of the greengrocers.

ANGIE. Well next time, have a look in the butcher's bins for us.

She turns away and closes the door. Chrissie empties the bag of sprouts over the heads of the geese.

2. Interior. Miss Sutcliffe's living room/kitchen. Day.

A gramophone is playing 'This Is My Lovely Day'. We see a dining table. A woman with her back turned is standing and moving away from the table, which is laid out for a now completed breakfast. We see a bowl of wheatmeal cobs, granary bread, a butter dish, an expensive coffee

*pot and a single used cup and saucer. The centre of the table holds
muesli, honey, high-powered marmalade and a splendid bowl of fruit. On
the far side of the table another place has been set for breakfast, but not
used. And the handsome, late middle-aged manageress of the Fraud
Section, Miss Sutcliffe, crosses to the sink with her plates. She then goes
to the mirror, looks, then crosses to the fridge/freezer which is casually
well stocked. She takes out a plastic bag full of salad, leaves that on the
cupboard surface, then crosses to the inevitably well-stocked wine-rack for a
bottle which she slips into the bottom of the fridge. It is as if she does this every
day of the week. She goes out into the hall to collect her post. A door opens at the
day of the week. She goes out into the hall to collect her post. A door opens at top
of stairs, and we see see just a blur of white nightdress as someone scrambles
for the bathroom and closes the door. Like a ghost on the run. We hear the click
of the bathroom lock. The manageress throws the letters down on a trolley, and
looks towards the room that 'the ghost' had just come from. The door is open.
The manageress approaches it. We see she is in her stocking feet. She enters the
room.*

3. Interior. Bedroom. Day.

*The music is much louder in this room. There is a disarranged bed in
the room, with the covers on, and a soaking sheet with a rubber
underneath. Again as if she does this every day, the manageress takes the
wet sheets off the bed, puts them in a wicker basket and jams the lid
back on. She crossed to a box of tissues, takes some, wipes her hands and
drops the tissues in a bin. She crosses to the gramophone and switches it
off. The music stops. She goes.*

4. Interior. Corridor. Day.

*The manageress moves towards the main room and the bathroom. We
hear the sound of running water. She goes to the bathroom door, listens to
the water briefly, then half-heartedly tries the handle. She winces. Her
voice when she speaks is resigned.*

MISS SUTCLIFFE. . . . Mother.

She knocks on the door.

MISS SUTCLIFFE. Come on, Mother. Please.

She knocks again. And again.

MISS SUTCLIFFE. Mother! Mother you know I need to . . .

She looks down suddenly at her bare feet. There is water coming from underneath the door, onto her feet. She jumps back quickly and then comes forward again. She bangs on the door desperately, then tries to barge against it as the water keeps coming.

MISS SUTCLIFFE. Mother! Mother! Mother! Mother!

5. Interior. Bathroom. Day.

Miss Sutcliffe is out of view but we hear her shouting.

MISS SUTCLIFFE. Mother!

We hear Miss Sutcliffe's bangs and attempts to open the door. We see inside the bathroom. The water is running, but straight down the plughole. A very old lady in a nightdress is sitting on the floor pouring water out of a water jug carefully under the door. She starts laughing, an insane cackle.

6. Interior. Corridor. Day.

We come back to Miss Sutcliffe. She has stopped thumping the door. She puts her head against it, and stands listening to the mad cackle. She is standing in the wet.

7. Exterior. Back of Chrissie's house. Day.

Chrissie is sitting on a tea-chest cleaning a double-barrelled shotgun. The back door opens inwards. Angie, still in her coat, comes out. She sits down by him.

ANGIE. . . . I'm sorry.

CHRISSIE. It's all right. I'm getting used to it.

She looks at him.

You're giving me nothing but crap all the time these days.

She starts to reply and we hear several knocks on the front door. Chrissie barely registers them. We hear Angie inside the house, going through the hall to the front door, though she is now out of view.

ANGIE. All right, all right . . . *(She opens the front door, misses a beat.)* Chrissie!

He get up, leaving the gun in the yard.

8. Interior. Back kitchen through to hall. Day.

As he enters the house she is already sweeping past him into the back kitchen. She speaks as she crosses him.

ANGIE. It's your comrades in crime . . .

Loggo and Malloy enter. Malloy closes the door. They stand just in the doorway. Loggo is already shame-faced. Chrissie slams the door that leads from the hall to the kitchen.

CHRISSIE. *(Immediately.)* Y'jokin' aren't y'?

MALLOY. What do you mean?

CHRISSIE. Coming here. That's really smart, that is. Did you bring him?

Loggo nods.

So that's what friends are for. Thanks Loggo, thanks a lot – now take him away. Far away.

LOGGO. Hang on, hang on.

MALLOY. Listen Chrissie . . .

CHRISSIE. Are y' sure it's not Kenny or Benny or Arthur or Frank?

MALLOY. Chrissie . . .

CHRISSIE. How about Veronica?

MALLOY. Oh, look. You're not being—

CHRISSIE. Look you, plums – me an' him 're in front of the Fraud Section this mornin' because of you – our Snowy got killed because of you . . .

MALLOY. Ah steady on now, that's not . . .

CHRISSIE. Because of you, I've had my dole stopped, I'm up to here in debt, I can't support my family, my wife's givin' me shite, *(We see Angie open the kitchen door.)* and for all I know I'll be up in court and down the road. Because of you.

MALLOY. Y'mean I kidnapped you and made you work for me – third slave to the right on the rowing boat?

CHRISSIE. All y' had to do, Malloy, was t'stop goosin' me on the side and make an honest man out of me, that's all, y'bastard. Now go on, get out.

Chrissie goes into the lounge. They follow.

LOGGO. Chrissie . . .

CHRISSIE. Y'can call me Kenny if y' want, Loggo.

MALLOY. Y'being unfair to me. And I've suffered as well. They're makin' me bankrupt, I'll go down before you—

CHRISSIE. Aaaahhhhhhhhh.

MALLOY. And I know y' not listenin' to me. I accept that. But for once, do yourself a favour and . . .

Chrissie walks to the front door and opens it, waiting for them to leave. Chrissie turns away.

CHRISSIE. I am doin'. I'm ignorin' y'. And remember this, I don't even want to see you ever again.

Chrissie goes out of the lounge back into the hall. They follow.

MALLOY. Chrissie, forty notes a day, in your hand, sound as a pound . . .

Chrissie goes towards the kitchen.

CHRISSIE. *(Loud.)* Where did I put me gun, Ange?

MALLOY. *(Giving up. He looks outside.)* All right, all right, can you get anyone else, Loggo?

LOGGO. Yeah, *(Looking away.)* I'll try, you know.

MALLOY. Monday mornin', Cazeneu Street, eight o'clock.

LOGGO. Yeah yeah.

Malloy looks out carefully, then departs. As he gets in his car, Loggo goes to follow him but glances towards the kitchen door. We see Chrissie staring at him from the dining-room door.

CHRISSIE. You soft get.

Loggo goes. Chrissie turns and opens the kitchen door. Inside the kitchen Angie is sitting on a stool. He goes to the sink, while she closes door.

ANGIE. So I'm givin' y' shite, am I?

CHRISSIE. Oh Jesus . . .

Angie crosses to him.

ANGIE. After what you did. Look!

CHRISSIE. I've already looked.

ANGIE. Look again.

She holds up a bread wrapper.

ANGIE. No bread. For breakfast. The kids' breakfast.

CHRISSIE. Oh come on, Angie. We've already talked about it –

He goes to the door.

ANGIE. No we didn't talk about it – you threw a moody and went out there . ... *(He walks away. She follows.)* to talk to the animals . . . Doctor Doolittle all right. *(Chrissie looks away.)* There was bread last night.

CHRISSIE. Three slices. Angie. Three stale slices.

ANGIE. Yes. And you ate them.

CHRISSIE. No, I sandpapered the ceiling with them.

(He goes out into the hall and leans on the banister.)

ANGIE. You ate them, and it was the kids' breakfast.

CHRISSIE. Oh don't. Just don't. How much guilt can I take, eh girl? Go on, where d' you go from bread – how about breadwinner'? Hey, hey? That's what y' really sayin', isn't it? 'Bread . . . winner'.

She throws the breadwrapper at him and turns her back on him.

CHRISSIE. I'm going out.

He puts his coat on. Angie leans out into the hall from the kitchen.

ANGIE. Where y'going?

CHRISSIE. Sell me arse on Lime Street. After all, I've tried everything else . . .

He goes out of the front door. She leans against the kitchen door frame.

9. Interior. Department of Employment. Main hall. Day.

We see a high establishing shot of the body of the main hall, with claimants queueing and the counter-clerks at work.

10. Interior. Fraud Section office. Day.

We see the manageress of the Fraud Section office, Miss Sutcliffe, plus her assistant in the leather jacket from Episode Two. The office has two desks, four chairs, two telephones on each desk, filing cabinets, a few charts and a large map of Greater Merseyside. Plus a semi-tropical forest of potted plants on every possible ledge and window sill. Both Miss Sutcliffe and her assistant are on the phone, but as the scene starts the assistant puts his down and begins to write. Miss Sutcliffe is writing on a note pad as she talks.

MISS SUTCLIFFE. . . . And your name, if I may? . . . Ah yes, Minnie Mouse. Your brother Mickey often phones us up.

She puts the phone down and talks almost to herself, with amused contempt, as there is a knock on the door.

MISS SUTCLIFFE. Along with Robert Redford, Elsie Tanner, several characters out of 'The Perishers' and Pope John Paul the Second . . . Come in. *(The door opens.)* We even had a Tallulah Bankhead once.

We see it is Lawton and Jackie Mills, the driver out of Episode One and the perfume representative out of Episode Two.

MISS SUTCLIFFE. Ah yes. Yes? You want my permission to get married?

They laugh. Lawton slightly too much.

MILLS. Could we see you for a few moments please, Miss Sutcliffe?

MISS SUTCLIFFE. Certainly. How about tomorrow.

LAWTON. It's, er, about our expenses, Ma'am.

MISS SUTCLIFFE. Oh well, make it the day after tomorrow then.

She smiles in dismissal, looks away, then looks back in surprise.

LAWTON. But, er, the day after tomorrow's Saturday.

MISS SUTCLIFFE. Yes, I know.

Miss Sutcliffe smiles blissfully. Lawton and Mills go to turn away with maiming on their mind. Miss Sutcliffe looks at her note pad.

MISS SUTCLIFFE. Oh Miss Mills, here's a little something for you – a lady in Charlotte Street – perhaps you could interest her in some perfume from your catalogue?

Miss Sutcliffe again smiles at Mills, who smiles back until Miss Sutcliffe looks down at her note pad, at which point Miss Mills' lip curls. As it were.

MISS SUTCLIFFE. She's been accused of – erm – let me see . . . prostitution, cohabitation, mass murder, drug smuggling, and a leading role in the Afghanistan Rebellion. *(She holds out the piece of paper from her note pad.)* The informant is a person by the name of Ms Minnie Mouse.

Mills takes the paper.

MILLS. Isn't that more likely to be a case for Social Security? Their Fraud Section.

MISS SUTCLIFFE. *(Thinks carefully.)* . . . Yes.

MILLS. Well, why are you giving it to me then, Miss Sutcliffe?

Miss Sutcliffe looks shocked and disapproving.

MISS SUTCLIFFE. Yours not to reason why, yours but to do or die. My dear.

Mills turns away from her and approaches Lawton at the door.

MISS SUTCLIFFE. Oh incidentally, Lawton, my deepest commiserations on failing your driving test. *(He looks at her and then away.)* Again.

LAWTON. Er, yes . . . er, thank you, Miss Sutcliffe.

They both go out, leaving the door open in their haste. Miss Sutcliffe smiles happily at her assistant as he goes towards the door, and glances out into the corridor before closing the door.

MISS SUTCLIFFE. Yes, she has got a nice pair of legs, hasn't she . . . I don't care very much for those two. I don't know why.

ASSISTANT. *(Flatly.)* They catch people.

MISS SUTCLIFFE. Ah, I knew there was a reason.

She looks across the room at the assistant, inviting comment. She doesn't get any. There is a knock on the door, immediately followed by the door opening. We see Donald Moss, Lawton's associate in Episode One, as he flurries into the room.

MOSS. Excuse me, sorry to bother you, apologies for the disturbance.

Moss grabs a chair, sits down, folds his arms.

MISS SUTCLIFFE. Well?

MOSS. No, I just thought I'd give your memory a little jog. You know – *(Points to himself.)* – Donald Moss, mid-thirties, two children, house in Haydock, Fraud Section Investigator, never a high flyer but just about where he should be in the scheme of things, comes to work every morning, sits in his office . . . and waits. And waits.

MISS SUTCLIFFE. You can leave. Would you like to leave? It can be arranged.

Miss Sutcliffe and her Assistant exchange glances. She gets up and goes to pour herself some coffee.

MOSS. The only reason I'm here is because I don't want to be queueing out there.

MISS SUTCLIFFE. That's the only reason any of us are here, Donald. *(She gives him a cup of coffee, and returns to her desk.)* Without them, most of us would be without a job. Correct, Derek?

ASSISTANT. Pardon?

Miss Sutcliffe shakes her head.

MISS SUTCLIFFE. *(Confidentially.)* Actually, I'm saving you for a very special assignment, Donald.

MOSS. . . . And?

MISS SUTCLIFFE. We haven't got one at the moment.

MOSS. You're doing this to me on purpose. You are, aren't you? Why?

Miss Sutcliffe sits.

MISS SUTCLIFFE. Can I ask you something?

MOSS. Only if it's worth answering.

MISS SUTCLIFFE. Do you like . . . catching people?

We see the Assistant Manager staring dolefully.

MOSS. . . . That's got nothing to do with it.

MISS SUTCLIFFE. Oh but it has. A lot to do with it.

MOSS. No it hasn't. It's a job. I got given it, it was looked on as promotion, and I'm doing it. Or in this instance – not doing it.

MISS SUTCLIFFE. But you're a nice man, Donald.

He stands up and crosses to her desk, fast.

MOSS. Oh go and! . . . Look. The last assignment I had was two weeks ago. The builder – the feller falling out of the window – since then, nothing.

Miss Sutcliffe sighs.

MISS SUTCLIFFE. . . . Come – *(She throws it in fast.)* – Come up and see me sometime. No, well alright, come back later. An hour or so. And I promise I'll have found something for you to do. In the meantime . . . I think your blotting paper calls . . .

She turns away from him. He hesitates angrily for a second or so and then slams out of the room. The assistant looks sick.

MISS SUTCLIFFE. I really like Donald when he's angry, he's ever so sweet. *(There is a pause.)* You're right, you don't have to tell me. I am a cranky frustrated mature spinster employed as a kind of . . . creeping jesus sprat-catcher . . . living with an almost completely insane mother . . . and I am a woman who has recently become aware of the massive and total futility of her life.

ASSISTANT. Ah now, come on. We agreed, didn't we – remember, we wouldn't talk about our personal problems.

MISS SUTCLIFFE. You mean *my* personal problems . . . It's all right. I will retire next year . . . and my mother will die soon. *(She turns away from him towards her desk.)* I've made up my mind . . .

The phone rings on his desk. He picks it up and listens.

ASSISTANT. Yes . . . No, I don't need to know your name.

He reaches for pen and paper.

11.   Exterior. Building site. Day.

Loggo and Chrissie are walking through a building site, full of half-

completed houses. Loggo is having to walk quickly to keep up with Chrissie.

CHRISSIE. *(Angrily.)* . . . You're mad, you are. Mad. We're both gettin' followed, for all we know, we're both goin' t'get prosecuted f'doin' a foreigner while we're on the dole . . .

LOGGO. But the . . .

CHRISSIE. And here you are, cool as a cucumber, startin' work f'Malloy of all people, and f'pound notes. What are y'trying t'do to y'self?

LOGGO. I've got no money.

CHRISSIE. Oh well, that explains everythin'.

LOGGO. An' I'm havin' a bad time with the HP – all those friggin' instalments.

CHRISSIE. Send the stuff back then.

CHRISSIE. I would if I could, but I've sold most of it already . . . and I'm months behind with the rent.

CHRISSIE. Move in with y' mam an' dad.

LOGGO. I can't do that – they still think I'm a virgin – pick up a creamie an' where could I take her for a bit of recreation? Besides they're in more debt than I am.

CHRISSIE. Well just sod off then, Loggo. I've got my own troubles, I don't need yours.

Loggo stops astonished. He looks at Chrissie striding away. Chrissie stops.

CHRISSIE. Yeah well. *(A silent apology.)* I'm worried sick.

Loggo follows him and gets level.

LOGGO. Worryin' 'll do no good. Me Uncle Matthew was a hypochondriac – never out of the X-ray unit at the Royal – barium this an' barium that – got killed by lightnin'.

CHRISSIE. All I want's a job, Loggo. An outside job.

LOGGO. Be careful, that's what me Uncle Matthew had.

They are by the site agent's hut which is only a few yards away. Chrissie looks at Loggo.

CHRISSIE. Everythin's a joke to you, isn't it?

Chrissie goes in. We focus on Loggo who quietly mimics the scene inside.

LOGGO. *(Leaning on wall.)* 'Anythin' goin' boss?' 'Sorry son, nothin'.'

Loggo clicks his fingers and points at the door. Sure enough, Chrissie comes out on cue. Loggo gets no satisfaction though.

LOGGO. Any job?

CHRISSIE. Oh aye, yeah, but I turned it down – didn't fancy the company car . . .

Chrissie walks off. Loggo tries to keep up with him.

LOGGO. Y'know your trouble – everythin's a joke to you . . .

12.   Interior. Fraud Section office. Day.

Yosser is in the middle of a speech and clearly on his way towards breakdown. He is speeding more than ever. As he talks, the manageress is looking at her assistant, who looks at his desk. Then they both look at their watches. Yosser's children are also present: Dustin at the window, Jason by the anglepoise lamp and finally his daughter by a filing cabinet, where she is opening a drawer.

YOSSER. *And* – and on Malloy's site that particular day, the day in question, in fact, no money parted company to or from anyone. Who was there. When I was there. No money came my way. Not to my knowledge. Not when I was there. And I should know. Being there. And being me. *(He laughs, and stops dead.)* Malloy on no occasion never said to me, 'Here y'are, touch for that'. *(Makes a movement with his hand indicating money being passed.)*

ASSISTANT. That's a double negative.

YOSSER. Yeah well, there's two of you isn't there? And, as a matter of fact, I was there on a trial basis, but left after one wobbly wall and a short exchange of words, or words to that effect.

MISS SUTCLIFFE. Mr Hughes, nobody is—

YOSSER. Look, here I am, a man. *(He laughs.)* A man. A man. With no job. Looking for one. *(He laughs again.)* It's like tryin' t'find the Scarlet Pimpernel. *(He moves in.)* Have you got a job, gizza job, eh, I'd be alright, if I had a job. Honest. *(He sits.)* I'd be alright. *(He shouts.)* Oh yes.

> *During the following speech the manageress goes to the door, opens it and looks out. Loggo and Chrissie are leaning against a wall outside the door. She closes the door on them and on her way back she gently closes the filing cabinet and moves the girl away. Yosser seems finally to have run out of steam. She stands by the cabinet.*

MISS SUTCLIFFE. Well. That has been very . . . long, Mr Hughes. I don't think we need to trouble you any further.

> *Yosser sits there.*

You were, after all, only asked here to help our enquiries.

> *And Yosser sits there.*

If you would like to go. Away. *Now.* Thank you.

> *Yosser stands. He walks towards the door and opens it. The children file out. Loggo and Chrissie are waiting still. Yosser addresses them sanely as he goes out.*

YOSSER. You're alright boys, you're sound, y'can kid them soft . . . *(He laughs.)*

> *Loggo and Chrissie move towards the door, but Miss Sutcliffe closes the door on them again. She looks at her watch and at the assistant and crosses to sit in front of him. Then she takes her shoe off.*

MISS SUTCLIFFE. How time flies when you're . . . Now, I know this is very naughty Derek, and after all it is your case, but I think we'll see the next two together.

ASSISTANT. What?

MISS SUTCLIFFE. I know, I know, protocol and rules, memos

from above, firm directives from the Ministry. But no one will
know except us, and I'm not going to tell anybody.

*She gets up and opens the door. The assistant throws down his pad in
disgust.*

Come in, gentlemen . . .

Chrissie and Loggo enter the Fraud Section office.

13. Exterior. Front of Chrissie's house. Day.

*Two men are standing outside of Chrissie's house at the front door. They
knock. The door half opens. We see Angie. She looks at the men, then at
the cards they are flourishing. She slams the door fast.*

GAS MAN. Go an' get a chisel, Jimmy . . .

*One man turns away and gets a tool-box from the van. Angie has run
round to the lounge window. When she looks out and sees the mate
return with his tool-box, she bangs the window.*

ANGIE. No. Wait.

She returns to the hall and opens the door to let them in.

14. Interior. Fraud Section office. Day.

*Miss Sutcliffe is at her desk. Her assistant, in his leather jacket, is
closing his note pad, in the centre of his desk. Miss Sutcliffe is slightly
distanced from him. He shuffles his papers with an air of finality and
puts his pen away. Loggo and Chrissie are sitting at the other side of the
desk, looking suitably muted. As well as blank. They all stare at each
other for a couple of seconds. Both 'couples' exchange looks.*

ASSISTANT. *(Formally.)* I think that just about concludes
everything.

LOGGO. Er yeah. Er all that y've just said, y'know, the mumbo
jumbo – what it means is er . . . what does it mean?

The assistant sighs with great contempt. Miss Sutcliffe intervenes, speaking pleasantly.

MISS SUTCLIFFE. I'm sorry, we didn't intend to confuse you. What my colleague is saying is that it is his intention to forward your papers for prosecution.

LOGGO. Y'goin' to do us then?

MISS SUTCLIFFE. Well it certainly looks that way, gentlemen.

LOGGO. Ah, she called me a gentleman, now isn't that nice. Chrissie.

CHRISSIE. Leave it alone, will y'.

MISS SUTCLIFFE. Wise advice.

ASSISTANT. In your situation.

MISS SUTCLIFFE. It would be even wiser to listen to it, Mr Logmond.

ASSISTANT. And no doubt impossible for you.

LOGGO. Friggin' hell, this is a double act. Or else one's a ventriloquist.

ASSISTANT. That's enough.

LOGGO. 'Enough' – from what you've been sayin' it hasn't even started yet. I thought y' would have had y' pound of flesh when y' killed Snowy Malone.

Chrissie sighs.

ASSISTANT. He killed himself.

LOGGO. Oh aye, yeah. He was always jumpin' from third floor windows – it was his hobby.

ASSISTANT. None of this behaviour is helping you, you know.

LOGGO. I wish I was hard. I mean I wish I had a leather jacket like that to make me hard.

ASSISTANT. Just don't.

LOGGO. Why – what are you going to do about it.

CHRISSIE. Forget it.

LOGGO. State of it though Chrissie – had to stand on a stool t'reach manhood.

CHRISSIE. Y'askin' f'trouble.

LOGGO. Well. We've already got it, haven't we – so screw them.

He turns to the assistant.

All right, go on, go 'head do what y'please – see if I care, only I'm telling you just don't walk home alone in the dark, that's all.

ASSISTANT. I hope, for your sake, that's not a threat.

Loggo shakes his head. When he replies, he does so quietly.

LOGGO. It's a promise.

Miss Sutcliffe stands.

MISS SUTCLIFFE. If I could bring the matter to a close, Mr Logmond, Mr Todd, before tempers get too heated. *(She crosses to the door.)* We will keep you informed of the . . . eventualities of this particular case, but . . .

LOGGO. Yeah yeah, all right. Don't bother trying to be nice, eh. It doesn't go with y' job. But at least there's one savin' grace – we won't have you minge bags followin' us around anymore, like bad smells.

ASSISTANT. *(Eager to score any kind of point.)* I wouldn't count on that, if I were you.

LOGGO/CHRISSIE. You wha'?

Chrissie stands up.

CHRISSIE. What? What for?

ASSISTANT. Because of your known and undenied activities, to possibly further the strength of our case . . . and as a deterrent. To you, and the likes of you.

CHRISSIE. What's your name? Hey? Come on, what's your name?

ASSISTANT. Why?

Chrissie crosses to the assistant.

CHRISSIE. Why? Because I'm going to report you that's why?

ASSISTANT. It won't do you any good.

LOGGO. *(Quietly.)* I know what will though . . .

CHRISSIE. *(Leaning over.)* No one's followin' me anymore, I'm tellin' y'. No one. Havin' a job's one thing – I'm sure it must make you very proud – but usin' it to persecute people's another. 'Cos that's what y' doin'. Now what's your name?

MISS SUTCLIFFE. Gentlemen, gentlemen.

LOGGO. There she goes again.

CHRISSIE. *Tell me your name.*

LOGGO. Come on, we've told you ours, it's only fair. Play the white man, will y'.

CHRISSIE. I want your name.

LOGGO. So do I. An' that's just for starters.

LOGGO. Give us your friggin' name!

ASSISTANT. . . . I don't want to, and I'm not going to. It's not . . . advisable.

Miss Sutcliffe takes over.

MISS SUTCLIFFE. Absolutely correct and proper, although you can have my name if you like, you can even have my address – however, do not hesitate to register a formal complaint – gentlemen – if you feel you have not been treated in a fitting manner. But I do really suggest that our interview is now over.

She moves to the door, smiling warily at them.

ASSISTANT. For the time being.

Loggo and Chrissie hesitate. Chrissie turns to the assistant.

CHRISSIE. I wouldn't be you. *I wouldn't be you.* Not for anythin'.

They move towards the door and go out. As they go Chrissie says 'Fascist Bastards'.

Inside the Fraud Section office, there is a pause before Miss Sutcliffe closes the door.

ASSISTANT. Scum.

MISS SUTCLIFFE. . . . Oh I don't think so, Derek.

ASSISTANT. I do. If they had brains they'd be dangerous.

MISS SUTCLIFFE. Now you may be right there. But there again, that could apply to more than those two.

He goes to the filing cabinet. She goes into the alcove.

ASSISTANT. . . . Meaning?

MISS SUTCLIFFE. Just a general comment on mankind . . .but . . . *(And re-enters from the alcove with a plant spray.)* As I'm in charge of this deliberately feeble attempt at a Fraud Section, I think I should tell you straight away that I do not intend to let the case against those two go forward.

She waters the plant on her desk.

ASSISTANT. You're what?

MISS SUTCLIFFE. I'm not going to let the case against those two go forward.

She waters the plant on the filing cabinet.

ASSISTANT. I've spent hours – days – this was my case.

MISS SUTCLIFFE. It was, yes.

She goes out. He slams the filing cabinet closed and follows.

15. Interior. Corridor to main hall. Day.

She goes out into the corridor, he follows, they walk.

MISS SUTCLIFFE. That builder, whatisname.

ASSISTANT. Malloy.

MISS SUTCLIFFE. Malloy, I think we'll have him. Put someone on him, would you, Derek, keep me in touch, as soon as he moves we'll jump, all right? After all, he's the really naughty boy, practically making a profession out of it. I don't mind prosecuting him at all. But those two – no . . . The black boy was rather pretty though, don't you think? In a rather coarse sort of way.

ASSISTANT. You can't mean that.

MISS SUTCLIFFE. About the black boy?

ASSISTANT. No. About not prosecuting. Them.

MISS SUTCLIFFE. Oh but I do.

They reach the main hall. She turns away from him. She goes through the doorway into the area behind the grilles and closes the door.

15a. Interior. Inside the counter area. Day.

They continue walking.

ASSISTANT. But why not?

MISS SUTCLIFFE. Why not? Really?

ASSISTANT. Yes.

MISS SUTCLIFFE. I can hear the laughter and outrage now. First of all, we manage to crash all our vehicles into a council wagon at the start of the raid, then a man is killed who is only killed, whatever we might say, because he is trying to escape from us, and finally for good measure, we are trying to arrest unemployed men who are busy building an unemployment exchange.

She laughs.

We see Moss in his office. They reach him, and she goes in. When she speaks to Moss it is infuriatingly like a loving mother to a young child. She waters the plants in his office as she talks.

MISS SUTCLIFFE. I haven't kept you waiting long, have I?

MOSS. Oh no, what's three-quarters of an hour to a man who's been wasting his time for some weeks.

MISS SUTCLIFFE. My thoughts exactly. And ten more minutes won't make much difference, will it?

She walks straight past him and moves back towards the door. He gets up and goes to follow her. She closes it on him.

MISS SUTCLIFFE. But don't go away, I think I might have the very thing for you.

He is left looking through the glass after her.

16. Interior. Chrissie's back kitchen. Day.

We see a close up of Angie, who is full of loathing. She and Chrissie are sitting on stools, facing out.

ANGIE. Where were y'? *Where were y'?* Why didn't you tell me?

CHRISSIE. I forgot.

ANGIE. *You forgot?* You forgot they were coming to turn off the gas?

CHRISSIE. I had other things on my mind.

Angie goes to the sink, leans out, then turns.

ANGIE. Yeah well . . . it doesn't matter does it? We didn't have anything to cook anyway.

She throws the fridge door open.

Half a tub of marg, Monday's milk and a pound of dead lettuce.

CHRISSIE. That's all right, we'll save on the electricity.

Chrissie switches the fridge off at the wall plug.

They move into the hall.

ANGIE. Until they come to cut that off.

She storms past him to go up the stairs.

17. Interior. Chrissie's stairs and landing. Day.

Chrissie is following Angie up the stairs.

CHRISSIE. Yeah. Yeah! Until they come and cut that off. And then there won't be anything left to cut off will there except me. But they can't cut me off though, can they – that's your department.

ANGIE. I can't cut off what you haven't got.

She goes into the toilet. Fast. Chrissie reaches the toilet door, tries to open it, but then turns away.

CHRISSIE. I didn't think you could hurt me anymore.

He leans against the door.

But there again, practice makes perfect.

We hear Angie's voice through the door.

ANGIE. Not in your case.

Chrissie leans against the doorframe.

CHRISSIE. Do you sit around all day thinking these things up? Oh that's a good one – that'll hurt him . . .

ANGIE. No, I sit there and wait for you to do something. You've got to do something.

Chrissie bangs on the toilet door.

CHRISSIE. I *am* doing something. I'm going to court. Then I'm going to get a heavy fine. *(He is walking back and forth.)* Then I'll go to jail. *(He kicks the bedroom door.)* Do not stop. And you can go and live with your mother – an event you've been looking forward to for some time.

ANGIE. You know nothing about me, Chrissie.

CHRISSIE. No, y' right, y'right I don't. Of course I don't. If I'd have known you better, I would have known that. But I have this ability to live with someone for eleven years and not know anything about them. And of course, not knowing anything about you or anything come to that, I don't know what love is neither, do I.

Angie laughs from the safety of the toilet.

Well it obviously isn't an empty fridge and the gas cut off.

The toilet flushes. Angie comes out again. Chrissie is in her way.

ANGIE. Let me go past.

CHRISSIE. And when we get evicted, we'll be standing there in the street well and truly finished with each other. If that's what love's about.

He lets her go past into the bedroom where she straightens the bed.

It's not my fault, you know. *Not my fault.*

ANGIE. Self pity, that's all I've heard from you for months. And it's pitiful.

He follows her and grabs her arm. He speaks with strength and anger.

CHRISSIE. Look, Angie – go away, go to your mother's, go to y'sister's, go to the dogs for all I care – but go away. I'd rather have nothing than what I'm getting now. And go on your own if y' want. You don't have to take the kids and look the martyr.

He throws her on the bed.

If you wanna go, go. And hurry up about it.

Chrissie goes into their bedroom. Closes the door behind him. Angie looks at the door.

18.   Interior. Fraud Section office. Day.

Miss Sutcliffe is sitting at her desk. She presses the intercom. The Assistant Manager is sitting gazing out of the window.

MISS SUTCLIFFE. I'm free to take the usual heavy breathing now, Jean.

She puts the intercom off, and glances at her watch.

Though I could do with some lunch . . .

She looks across at her assistant.

You're still upset about my decision, aren't you?

She gets up and crossed to the alcove. The assistant is clicking his pen.

ASSISTANT. . . . Yes. You'll make me look a fool if this gets out.

MISS SUTCLIFFE. It won't 'get out', and just think of the joy you will bring into the lives of those two men when they find out.

He looks joylessly at her.

But I'll tell you what I'll do – just to make you happy – I'll put my little friend Donald on their tracks. Pass the time for them all.

She goes back in. The assistant gets up and crosses to join her.

ASSISTANT. But Moss was in on the arrest.

She is watering plants.

MISS SUTCLIFFE. Exactly.

ASSISTANT. They know each other.

MISS SUTCLIFFE. Precisely.

ASSISTANT. But for God's sake, that's illogical!

MISS SUTCLIFFE. So, my dear boy, is God. We're chasing people with nothing – who only want a little. Be a Christian, sport.

She misses a beat.

He really is a pleasant fellow, Moss, do you like Moss? I'm sure he'll find a different occupation eventually.

ASSISTANT. But what about his safety?

The intercom buzzes.

MISS SUTCLIFFE. Oh they wouldn't hurt him, they're nice boys.

ASSISTANT. . . . Are you . . . sending me up?

She crosses out of the alcove.

MISS SUTCLIFFE. Good heavens no, Derek. What on earth makes you think that?

He does not reply.

She picks up the telephone, then sits down.

MISS SUTCLIFFE. Of course I don't know who you are, Sir, and I wouldn't dream of asking your name, Mr - - - ah! That's a new one. Well I never! Norman Tebbit . . .

19. Interior. Chrissie's landing. Day.

Angie walks up the stairs and stands outside their bedroom door. Chrissie is in the bedroom. They talk to each other through the door.

ANGIE. . . . How long're you going to stay in there?

CHRISSIE. Till you go away.

ANGIE. Ah Chrissie, you don't really want me to go away.

CHRISSIE. That's exactly what I want.

ANGIE. Right. I'm going then.

CHRISSIE. Good.

She crosses to the stairs and starts to go down.

ANGIE. You can have all the benefits.

Chrissie laughs.

I'll leave the family allowance book.

Chrissie laughs louder.

Yeah, so it's funny, is it Chrissie? Just see how far they get you. You're always tellin' me I can't make it stretch.

The door opens. Chrissie is standing there.

CHRISSIE. Go away!

The door slams in Angie's face as she runs up the stairs and crosses to the bedroom. She tries the door.

ANGIE. I need a suitcase.

A brief pause. The door opens. Chrissie hurls a suitcase out, then closes the door.

ANGIE. It isn't big enough.

Another pause. The door opens again. One more suitcase comes flying out. The door shuts again.

ANGIE. My clothes are in the wardrobe.

She kneels and opens the suitcase. There is a pause, with noise. The door opens. A pile of Angie's clothing comes flying out onto the landing.

ANGIE. Great, great.

Chrissie goes back in. Angie starts throwing her stuff into the suitcase. Chrissie keeps bringing more out as he finds it.

ANGIE. Thank you. *(She dismisses a dress.)* Don't need that.

ANGIE. Remember this – you made me go.

CHRISSIE. I won't forget it.

ANGIE. Don't.

CHRISSIE. I won't.

ANGIE. Good.

CHRISSIE. Fine.

ANGIE. All right.

CHRISSIE. Right.

ANGIE. Just so long as you know.

He slams the door.

ANGIE. I'll take the kids if you want.

He opens the door.

CHRISSIE. I don't want anything from you – especially the pressures you give me. You'd think I was the only man round here without a soddin' job. Take a look around y', girl, we form the majority around here. Only some fellers are lucky enough to have wives who recognize that fact.

ANGIE. Alright. Right. If that's what you really believe, I'm finished.

CHRISSIE. I thought we were finished anyway. You don't pack your suitcase to go to the shops.

Angie slams a suitcase shut.

ANGIE. What would be the point of going to the shops?

CHRISSIE. No y' right, y' so right, y' always are – don't go the shops – go to friggin' hell. And don't come back!

He goes into the bedroom and slams the door. She goes down the stairs.

20. Interior. Chrissie's house. Day.

As the fight continues, there is a knock on the door. Angie puts the suitcases down and opens the door. Hanging onto the knocker, almost unconscious, is George in his hospital escape outfit.

ANGIE. Uncle . . .

She gets hold of him, and shouts.

Chrissie! CHRISSIE!

CHRISSIE. I'm not in.

ANGIE. It's y' Uncle George, y' stupid get!

She can't take George's weight anymore, and sits down on a suitcase which ludicrously collapses on her.

Oh Christ, George.

As Chrissie comes running down the stairs and lifts George off, she closes the door.

21. Interior. Fraud Section office. Day.

We see Moss, in close-up. He is in mid-seizure.

MOSS. But where's she gone?

ASSISTANT. She's gone to lunch.

MOSS. I've been stood outside the flaming door. How could she?

The assistant looks down, mumbles into his midriff.

ASSISTANT. She went out the window.

MOSS. *What?*

He looks towards the ground floor windows in the alcove at the back of the room.

ASSISTANT. She went out of the window.

MOSS. Oh, go away.

ASSISTANT. She's been out the window for some time . . .

MOSS. Jesus . . . Is this her idea – to follow Logmond and Todd? *(The assistant nods.)* Of course. It's so absurd, it had to be. Look, I can't follow those two.

ASSISTANT. I know.

MOSS. Well, somethings got to be done.

ASSISTANT. I know. *I know.* But you know as well as I do that this is the Civil Service, and you have to rape a Junior Minister or eat the filing cabinets before you get—

MOSS. Promoted.

ASSISTANT. Whatever.

MOSS. And in the meantime I'm expected to play the tin can in a shooting gallery. *(The assistant shrugs.)* Knockout.

ASSISTANT. But if it's any consolation I've . . . and keep this to yourself . . . I've kept a file on her behaviour. *(He looks up at Moss, then looks quickly away.)* It's not a thing I wanted to do, but you don't see the half. I might have to sent it anonymously, but if this keeps up, I am going to send it. And I could need your support if any action is taken. Donald.

MOSS. That's the last thing you'll have. *(The assistant looks up sharply at him.)* 'Cos I won't be here. And I've got to go now, but it's all right, don't get up, don't worry, I'll find my own way out.

Moss goes over to the window, talking as he goes, opens the window and climbs out. He turns back to face the assistant.

MOSS. I've got two options left open to me now -- either to get pissed or follow those two. Perhaps I'll do both. Because I'll tell you frankly, and she was right, I hate this job.

Moss moves away from the window and walks off.

22.   Interior. Chrissie's living room. Day.

George is half lying, half sitting on the sofa. Chrissie is selflessly angry. With George.

CHRISSIE. I don't need your help – I don't want you here! What are you doin' coming here?

GEORGE. I heard. About you an' Loggo.

CHRISSIE. So?

Angie comes in with tea for George. Angie and Chrissie stand close together. Almost like a loving couple.

GEORGE. So I know what to do – I've been through this before with the dole. I'm becomin' an expert.

He tries to grin. She stands by Chrissie.

CHRISSIE. Yeah, on other people's behalf, but not mine, not this time, d' y'hear?

GEORGE. Aye, aye, Chrissie, no need to shout.

CHRISSIE. *(Calmly.)* Look, Uncle George, you come first. When y'not well, you yourself come first. I'm tellin' y' this for y' own good.

GEORGE. Oh sod that.

ANGIE. No, Chrissie's right.

GEORGE. If I'm treated like a sick old man I will be a sick man.

CHRISSIE. And if you carry on like this . . .

There is a knock on the front door. Angie goes to the front window.

GEORGE. I know, it's the ambulance. People are always doin' it for me. Out of the goodness of their hearts.

CHRISSIE. Come on.

Chrissie goes to help George, he helps him get up.

GEORGE. I'm O.K. I'll be alright.

Chrissie goes out with him.

CHRISSIE. Course y'will. And don't worry I'll sort it out. No sweat . . .

We see George and Chrissie leave the room. George is taken outside to the ambulance. Chrissie returns and there is silence as they stay at the window watching George get into the ambulance.

ANGIE. . . . It's not just family with George, is it – he does that for everyone, doesn't he?

CHRISSIE. The whole estate. All creeds and denominations. And cripples and failures and head-bangers. Open house. And what does he get for it and what's his reward? He gets so sick he's never going to get better and he loses his youngest son. *(He looks up.)* Thank you, Almighty God. Thank you. You work in mysterious ways alright. *(Angry.)* And none of them are worth a wank.

ANGIE. . . . You wouldn't have said that once.

CHRISSIE. Even altar boys grow up, Angie. And if you've ever believed in something, really believed in it and you find out it's not worth believing in, all you want to do is kick it till it's dead.

He pauses and looks at her.

But you know that, don't you. That's what you feel . . . about me.

23. Interior. Chrissie's lounge. Day.

ANGIE. You give me no option at times.

CHRISSIE. Nah, I'm the one with no options. Me dad used to say to me – 'Don't get mad – get even' . . . I can't even get mad these days.

He goes into the hall and picks up his coat off the banister. So does she.

ANGIE. You leavin' as well? We're both leaving now are we?

CHRISSIE. I'm going to see a man about a job and then I'm going to pick the kids up. Get some practice in for when you're not here.

He goes straight out without looking, leaving the door invitingly open.

24. Exterior. Front of Chrissie's house. Day.

We go outside the house. Chrissie is leaning against the wall a few yards away. He looks around at the house, pensively. We go back inside to see Angie standing by the suitcases, then she picks them up, goes to the door and closes it with one of the suitcases. She begins to walk up the stairs. Outside again, we see Chrissie leaning against the wall. He closes his eyes and breathes out. A car comes round the corner. We hear the noise of car brakes, not harsh, but stopping quickly. Then we see Moss getting out of a Marina. Chrissie stands by the wall on the corner, Moss approaches him. Moss has the desperate air of a man no longer in control and no longer caring.

MOSS. Hi! Remember me?

CHRISSIE. *(Bleakly.)* 'By the powers invested in me . . .'

MOSS. Got it in one. Well done.

CHRISSIE. It was nothin'. What d' y' want?

MOSS. You. I've got to follow you about. You and Logmond. No really. *(He looks around.)* You don't happen to know where he is, do you? I would be fairly grateful if you two kept together. It would make my job a lot easier. *(he smiles at Chrissie.)*

CHRISSIE. If this is a joke, I can supply the punch-line.

Chrissie, then Moss, start walking.

MOSS. No it's not joke, it's an outright madness. Now let me see, there's two of you, and only one of me, so if you insist on not being together, I'll have to follow you in turns. Who do you think should go first? Do you want to toss for it?

He searches in his pocket for a penny.

Oh and by the way, I won't be working nights or weekends.

They stop.

CHRISSIE. What's all this about?

MOSS. You know on Christmas Day in the First World War, when the enemy troops from both sides got together in No Man's Land and made friends and played football.

Chrissie stares at him.

And just for once forgot the absolute lunacy of what they were doing to each other?

CHRISSIE. . . . Yeah.

MOSS. Well. This is it, pal. This is Christmas Day.

He smiles at Chrissie.

MOSS. Oh. And don't worry, because I know something you don't know. You see, before long we're both going back behind the lines.

He winks at Chrissie and goes back to the car. When he reaches it he turns to face Chrissie. Chrissie looks confused.

MOSS. Happy New Year. Pal.

He gets in the car. Chrissie begins to walk away.

25.　Exterior/Interior. Moss's Car. Day

Moss is sitting in the car alone and only then do we see the abject hopelessness of the man. He looks around, his arms on his lap. He reaches for his CB microphone.

MOSS. No! No, no, no. Not me. This is Donald Moss.

He searches for things in his pocket.

Here's my warrant card.

He throws it down.

Me little tin badge.

He throws it down.

Here's my office keys and here's my plastic government issue briefcase . . . signing off.

He gets out of the car.

Oh, and here's the keys to the car. It's low on oil.

He walks towards the pavement.

I'd sooner be back on the counter. In Wigan.

He throws the keys down the drain.

26.　Interior. Chrissie's Living Room. Day.

Chrissie, Angie and their two children, Justin and Clare, aged ten and eight, all well wrapped up, are watching the end of the children's programmes on BBC-1, just before the early evening News. A small two-bar electric fire is in front of the gas fire. There is a ring at the door. Angie is nearest to the door and goes out. Chrissie follows to the lounge doorway. Angie opens the front door to Loggo and Malloy. Angrily, she comes back to the lounge, she doesn't look at Chrissie.

ANGIE. It's for you.

Chrissie crosses into the hall.

27. Interior. Chrissie's hall. Day.

He goes into the hallway, closing the sitting-room door. Malloy and Loggo are outside, anxious. There is a pause as Chrissie looks at them.

CHRISSIE. Y' got the message then?

Malloy nods.

. . . Yeah well, you'd better come in . . .

28. Interior. Chrissie's hall. Day.

As Malloy and Loggo are about to step inside the house, we see and hear a van pulling to a halt outside the house. It is driven by the Assistant Manager. Lawton, who is the passenger, bounces out eagerly and runs towards Chrissie's open door. The Assistant Manager gets out of the van as well. Chrissie tries to slam the door on Loggo and Malloy.

CHRISSIE. Oh shit.

Loggo and Malloy push in past him fast.

29. Interior. Chrissie's hall/passage to the back kitchen. Day.

Malloy tries to blunder into Chrissie's living room but is dragged back by Loggo, who pushes him into the kitchen. They wrestle and Loggo runs through the kitchen. Angie has come out into the hall.

ANGIE. What the hell . . .

At the front door, Chrissie tries to stop Lawton as he pushes at the front door and keeps it open.

LAWTON. Avon calling.

Loggo and Malloy run out the back. Lawton and the Assistant Manager follow, pushing arrogantly past Chrissie. They also push Angie aside.

ASSISTANT. Excuse me love.

Chrissie shouts.

30. **Exterior. Chrissie's back yard. Day.**

Loggo crashes into the back yard, followed by Malloy. They stop while Loggo opens Chrissie's back yard door. Waiting behind it are two heavy gentlemen. Loggo looks for escape desperately. He jumps over the goose pen and the side wall and out. Malloy, also trying to escape, turns back towards Lawton and the Assistant Manager, who come out of the house and takes hold of Malloy only. Loggo meets the second 'heavy' in the alley then turns and sees Lawton, the Assistant Manager and Malloy and the other two men. Loggo looks at them, then backs off, flinching slightly as they walk past, half expecting a clout. He runs off totally puzzled. Lawton and the Assistant Manager take Malloy along the alley.

MALLOY. (*Pathetically.*) But why me? What about them?

ASSISTANT. You're not pretty.

MALLOY. What?

ASSISTANT. Forget it.

They lead him away. Chrissie has moved a pace or two into the alley. He turns and walks back to the kitchen door. Angie slams it on him. He turns away.

31. **Interior. Miss Sutcliffe's flat. Evening.**

We see Miss Sutcliffe is at her dining table. The food she organized earlier in the day is on the table. So is the bottle of wine. She is on the phone. As the phone call continues we become aware that it is from her assistant.

MISS SUTCLIFFE. . . . yes I know, I know, it's fascinating, Derek, the three of them together. Indeed, in the same house at the same time. Perhaps they're friends, no? . . .

As her assistant talks, Miss Sutcliffe hears her mother's bedroom door open. She looks across. We see a salad dinner on a tray. A hand edges out from the bedroom and takes the tray slowly off the floor. The door closes. Miss Sutcliffe smiles bitterly.

MISS SUTCLIFFE. Yes Derek, no Derek, a coincidence, Derek, a mere accident of fate, time and event. And not to be pursued

. . . Just Malloy, that's my boy. *(She giggles.)* . . . Thank you anyway, Derek, but you will have to excuse me, I do have to go now. You see I'm very bored.

> *She puts the phone down, sits there, all malice and warmth, and begins to eat. She hears a window being opened in her mother's bedroom. Miss Sutcliffe stops eating and listens. There is a distant crash of crockery, seeming to be from outside. She looks to the dining room window, then to her mother's door. She approaches, opens the door gently and looks in. We see her mother's bedroom, one of the windows open wide, the curtains blowing and no sign of her mother. Miss Sutcliffe goes to the window quickly and looks out. Down below, on the ground, we see the remnants of the salad, the smashed plates, the teapot, the milk jug, and the cup. But no mother. Miss Sutcliffe looks around the room, focuses finally on a big old-fashioned wardrobe and approaches it. When she flings open both doors we see her mother in a nightgown, sitting in the bottom corner of the wardrobe with a quietly insane and victorious smile. Miss Sutcliffe slams both the doors shut, stares at the wardrobe for a second or two then turns the key to the doors of the wardrobe and locks them. She walks away.*

32. Interior. Chrissie's back kitchen/dining room. Evening.

Angie is collecting plates. She goes into the kitchen. Chrissie is there when she enters with three plates, knives and forks

CHRISSIE. Still not speakin' to me?

> *No answer, except she scrapes plates.*

Well, at least that's one question answered.

> *Angie moves back to collect the bread and bottles, and goes back into the kitchen to put them away.*

I thought you might have some comment to make about what happened before with Malloy. Even if it was just to express your disgust and contempt as . . .

ANGIE. I'd rather be starving.

She goes back into the dining room.

CHRISSIE. Oh great. Just like a woman. This afternoon is was my fault we were starving.

He follows.

But tonight you'd rather starve. Not that you have, though.

He goes back into the kitchen.

Does it amuse you not to make my tea? And then sit and sulk for three hours?

She turns away.

The best bit though was putting the kids to bed. Without sending them in to me. Leprosy as well, hey?

ANGIE. I hate you.

Angie goes into the lounge.

CHRISSIE. Of course you do. But it's alright. I don't mind, because you don't know anything about anything. You don't know y' arse from a hole in the ground – you – you think that life's like the inside of a Wendy House. And I'm only there to look after the dolls.

He follows her into the dining room, then into the lounge. She flies at him, fingernails to the front. Chrissie parries her attempts to scratch and hit him. He takes hold of her hands and is too strong for her. But he looks at her rage and her eyes.

CHRISSIE. Oh yeah. You as well, eh . . . Go on then. Why not, one free shot.

He lets go of her and stands there. Angie begins to batter him. she hits him in the face, on the chest and arms and shoulders, screaming. He falls back. She goes on battering him. He put his hands over his head in surrender.

ANGIE. For once in your life, stand up for yourself. Fight back. fight back . . .

She cannot carry on. She leans on arm of chair. Their younger daughter has appeared on the stairs. She is watching.

CHRISSIE. It's all right, Justine. Me and mummy are just playing at wrestling. And mummy's winning.

Angie still leans on the chair. Chrissie walks to the stairs, picks up Justine.

CHRISSIE. Hey come on, come on . . . we're only playing. Ssshh.

He takes Justine upstairs.

33. **Interior. Chrissie's living room. Evening.**

Angie is in a chair, with her back turned to the door. She is smoking a cigarette. Chrissie enters and closes the door.

CHRISSIE. She's asleep. And that's my last cigarette.

Angie throws it at him. It hits him but he ignores it, leaves it on the carpet. He sits down. They both look at the cigarette which is smouldering.

CHRISSIE. It's alright – I've stopped smoking.

ANGIE. So have I.

CHRISSIE. That's what I call a sudden decision.

There is a pause.

I'm not picking it up.

ANGIE. Neither am I.

CHRISSIE. You threw it.

ANGIE. You never caught it.

CHRISSIE. My dad's bigger than your dad.

ANGIE. I've got a big brother.

CHRISSIE. But I can fight him. Anyway, he's in Australia.

Chrissie smiles.

ANGIE. I'm not making friends.

Chrissie puts his finger to his lips and makes blubbering baby noises. She turns away from him.

ANGIE. You're not funny.

CHRISSIE. I'm not laughing.

Angie bends down and picks up the cigarette.

CHRISSIE. I thought you'd stopped.

ANGIE. Yeah well. I've started again.

CHRISSIE. No will-power, have you?

ANGIE. Oh! Sod off, Chrissie. I used to think you were funny, but not anymore.

CHRISSIE. Isn't it strange – I feel exactly the opposite about you. You're becoming more hysterical by the minute.

There is a long pause as Angie finishes the cigarette. Then she stubs it out.

CHRISSIE. Just like the home life of our gracious queen.

ANGIE. *Shut up*! I'm going to bed.

She stands up, strides off up stairs.

CHRISSIE. Is than an invitation?

Angie ignores him and goes out. He stops being funny immediately.

CHRISSIE. Obviously not . . .

Chrissie stands and goes over to where she was sitting. He inspects the cigarette end, and dismisses, reluctantly, the chances of smoking it. He walks back towards the couch, reaches out with his foot and boots the couch hard against the wall. As it hits the wall, the couch makes a jangling noise. He throws the cushions off. Chrissie looks at the couch in a new light. He tilts it on to its back. He hears the jangle of money again, and he rips the fabric off the seam at the bottom end. He puts his hand into the insides of the couch, feels around and brings out a crumpled packet of cigarettes. When he opens it and sees it is nearly full, he chuckles fit to bust. He puts them on top of the

sofa, then takes out half an ancient hamburger, some spilt chips,
several crayons, a few coppers and two 50p pieces. He tries to put
them on the sofa, fails and so puts them on the table. He rips the rest of
the bottom of the sofa off, finds a Liverpool FC programme, and
then to his sublime joy, a five-pound note. Almost infantile, certainly
childish in his pleasure, he holds it up to the light, inspects it and
kisses it.

34.   Interior. Bedroom. Night.

Angie is in bed, tossing and turning. She hears Chrissie singing
'Memories are made of this'.

35.   Interior. Chrissie's living room. Night.

Chrissie is lying on the sofa with a half-bottle of whisky and four cans
of lager, plus a huge portion of chips. He is just completing a demolition
job on the chips. He lifts the couch up and puts the chip paper down the side
of the sofa. He sings quietly 'Memories are made of this'.

36.   Interior. Bedroom. Night.

Angie is in bed as before. She hears Chrissie still singing.

37.   Interior. Chrissie's living room. Night.

We see the clock on the mantelpiece. It is quarter to seven and still dark
outside. We come back to Chrissie, who is asleep against the couch, but
just waking up. Around him are the lager cans and the empty whisky
bottle. He groans and sucks in his breath. He looks at the evidence of his
drinking, contemplates the base of the couch, but thinks better of it. He
gets to his feet, picking up the lager cans and whisky bottle. As he walks
into the hall, he drops a can on the floor.

38. Interior. Kid's bedroom. Night.

The kids are in bed together. One of them wakes up.

39. Interior. Hall. Night.

Chrissie bends down to pick up the can, and drops another. Then he drops the lot.

CHRISSIE. Frig it. Frig it.

He walks to the bottom of the stairs.

40. Interior. Chrissie bedroom. Night.

Angie has her back turned as Chrissie enters and starts to get undressed. The argument starts immediately. Throughout the scene he undresses, gets into bed, and as soon as he is in bed, the argument is such that he gets right out again and puts on his clothes.

CHRISSIE. Angie . . .

ANGIE. *What*? It's nearly seven o'clock, d'you know that?

CHRISSIE. Yeah, but . . .

ANGIE. You went out last night.

CHRISSIE. I know . . .

ANGIE. If you went for a drink I'll never talk to you again.

CHRISSIE. Promises, promises . . . No . . . I want to talk.

ANGIE. You are doing.

CHRISSIE. No . . .

ANGIE. I haven't slept.

CHRISSIE. I came up last night and you were fast.

ANGIE. I was pretending. I heard you, but I was pretending.

CHRISSIE. So was I. I never came up.

She turns away from him, covering the blankets around herself.

CHRISSIE. Angie. Angie. *Angie.*

She covers her head up now.

CHRISSIE. Angie. This is . . . our life . . . and I wish I was dead. But this is how it is at the moment. This is the way of our life . . .

He laughs, throwing the next sentence away.

It's a way of life. The only trouble is, it's no way to live. I know that . . . look, you don't have to go all miserable and bastard like and fight with me.

He gets into bed.

ANGIE. (*From beneath the bedclothes.*) You have been drinking.

Chrissie closes his eyes.

CHRISSIE. I had a job, Angie. It wasn't a bad job, and I was good at it. I laid the roads, girl. *I laid the roads.* Motorways, lay-bys, country lanes.

ANGIE. Chrissie . . .

CHRISSIE. No, no. Let me finish. I could tamper and grit like nobody you ever saw. Nobody put the black stuff down quite like me.

He shrugs.

But I lost that job, it was alright, I deserved to lose it, I was a dick-head – but haven't we all been at one time or another – haven't we all woken up the next mornin' an' gone 'oh Jesus, did I do that'? Yeah, well, once you could get away with it. But not now. That's the problem.

He lies back. Angie turns back to him, sits up in bed.

ANGIE. I am twenty-eight years old, Chrissie . . .

CHRISSIE. What's that got to do with?

ANGIE. No, look. Let me finish, alright. I am twenty-eight, I married you when I was seventeen. I was a mother at eighteen. Now I'm not blaming you for that, I'm not.

He lies under the covers.

ANGIE. It takes two to tango. But I'm a person you kn—

The alarm clock goes off at the side of the bed. She thumps it into silence.

ANGIE. - I live and breathe, and fart after five lager and limes. I have a mind up here. And it's screaming Chrissie. I mean it can't - it can't take much more. I mean, it was never much fun early on, how could it be . . . babies and sick and nappies and no sleep at nights - it's not like you imagine it to be, it's not like it is in the Woman's Own. But I loved you. I love the kids.

CHRISSIE. I like the past tense with me.

ANGIE. No no no. See, you never listen to me.

There is a pause. He sighs.

What I'm . . . the thing is . . . aaaaaaaahhhhhhhh! . . . I've never had a life outside of you and Justine and Clare. That's all. But I was going to. I was going to do a lot. Back to college. Job of my own. Out in the world. 'Hi Angie' . . . this was going to be my time. And what's happened instead - we're not, we're not even livin' hand to mouth.

CHRISSIE. All down to me, eh? Good old Chrissie, done it again.

ANGIE. No!

CHRISSIE. Absolute crap, Angie.

He gets out of bed and gets dressed fast and erratically.

Don't look at me if you're not going to college, don't look at me if you've got no life, don't.

Angie gets up in the bed.

ANGIE. Oh you, you, you. You never listen to me!

CHRISSIE. What is there to listen to?

ANGIE. So that's what you think - that's how much you know. And I'm the one who's supposed to know nothing! Well, not stood against you, I'm not.

CHRISSIE. Oh behave yourself - you're not even making sense.

ANGIE. What sense is there to make, Chrissie? What is it? What is there? What did I dream of - and where is it?

She points towards the children's bedroom.

What are they going to be doing in ten years' time? Are they still going to be wearing hand-me-downs at eighteen and twenty? What are we bringing them up for - and what is the point of livin' our lives when . . . when ye'get up in the mornin' and it's all downhill from then on . . . two ounces of spam and a quarter of brawn and any stale . . . look!

She grabs a shoe from the side of the bed, turns it so that the sole faces Chrissie, then realizes that it's the wrong one. She hurls it away, and gets the other one. Chrissie laughs. She shows him the shoe. There is a hole in the shoe, temporarily filled with cardboard.

ANGIE. Look -

CHRISSIE. Yeah, well. Walk on one leg, you'll be alright.

Angie pushes him on to the floor.

ANGIE. It's not funny, It's not friggin' funny. I've had enough of that - if you don't laugh, you'll cry - I've heard it for years - this stupid soddin' city's full of it - well, why don't you cry - why don't you scream - why don't you fight back, you bastard. Fight back. They're knockin' the shite an' stuffin' out of you, Chrissie Todd, and if you haven't had enough, I have.

CHRISSIE. . . . And what do you think it's like for me? Hey? A second class citizen. A second rate man. With no money and no job . . . and no . . . no place!

Angie turns away from him. She speaks flatly.

ANGIE. Tell it to the kids, Chrissie, tell it to the cupboards and the fridge. See how full y' words can make then. And when you've done that, make breakfast - and if y' do, y'll have found a job - because y'll have to be a soddin' magician.

Chrissie goes towards the door.

CHRISSIE. Yeah, I'll fill them, you see if I don't. I'll fill them -

and I hope you sodding enjoy it.

> *He crashes out of the room and down the stairs. We hear him*
> *banging into the back kitchen. We stay with Angie as she slumps on*
> *to the bed. We hear the kitchen door leading to the yard as it opens.*
> *We hear Chrissie crashing about. We see the children wake up. We*
> *see Angie looking up, then sitting up on the bed.*

41. Exterior. Chrissie's back yard. Dawn.

The children come to the window and look down as they hear Chrissie
coming out of the house and kicking a bucket. Chrissie throws the chickens
out of their pen into the yard. The children look out. Chrissie has
difficulty in getting all the chickens out. We see Angie join the children
at the window, then pull them away.

42. Interior. Landing. Chrissie's house. Dawn.

Angie pushes the children from their bedroom into the main bedroom. They are
both scared and shouting.

CHILDREN. What is he doing . . . is he hurting them . . . what is
he doing?

ANGIE. He's not doing anything . . . get in there and stay . . .

CHILDREN. What's he doing?

ANGIE. Get in . . . get in. Just get in. All right?

> *She closes the door on them and puts on her dressing-gown as she*
> *races down the stairs.*

43. Interior. Chrissie's back yard. Dawn.

The geese and the ferret are agitated. We see Angie arrive at the back door in her
dressing-gown, looking into the yard as Chrissie approaches. He has a cardboard
box in his arms. Chrissie empties the box so that the chickens and pigeons drop
limply around her feet.

CHRISSIE. Here y' are, chicken for a week, and as much pigeon pie as y' can eat.

Chrissie throws the box away, turns from Angie and lifts the gun. He loads it.

CHRISSIE. And goose for Sunday.

We see the geese. Angie moves to Chrissie's side, grabs hold of his arm. She keeps away from his range of fire as she tries to stop him.

ANGIE. Chrissie, don't. Jesus, don't.

He pushes her away to the back door and aims at the geese. We see them in their pen. Then we focus on Chrissie as he is about to pull the trigger. He fires both barrels. Feathers fly whilst the rabbits tremble. One of them has a substantial splattering of blood across its white fur. Chrissie looks around him. He cries out and hurls the gun away from himself. He sits on the tea chest, and cries and cries and cries. Slowly Angie moves towards him as he sits with his head in his hands, openly weeping. She goes down on her haunches, facing him, then puts her hands on his knees. She too is upset, and near to tears. He finally looks down at her hands, sees the blood and wipes it away. He tries to control himself and takes hold of her hands. He looks down at her, then looks slightly to her side, at the rabbit. He looks back. Eventually he speaks.

CHRISSIE. Somebody'd better wash the blood of that rabbit . . .

Angie half laughs, half cries at the ridiculousness of his words. After a time he joins her in laughter and tears. The action freezes.

Yosser's Story

YOSSER HUGHES Bernard Hill
MAUREEN HUGHES Jean Warren
JASON HUGHES Timothy Bleasdale
ANNE MARIE HUGHES Tamana Bleasdale
DUSTIN HUGHES Jamie Bleasdale
CHRISSIE TODD Michael Angelis
LOGGO LOGMOND Alan Igbon
GEORGE MALONE Peter Kerrigan
WINO James Ellis
DOCTOR Noreen Kershaw
PRIEST Struan Rodger
DOE CLERK Christopher Quinn
MOEY Peter Christian
SCHOOL ATTENDANCE OFFICER Terry Butler
HEALTH VISITOR Ian Clough

PUB MANAGER   Steven Faye
ELECTRICIAN   Joey Kaye
RENTMAN   Nick Maloney
MORGAN   Lloyd Peters
VERONICA   Lesley Nightingale
EVICTION MAN   John Chegwin
SCARFACE POLICEMAN   Harry Goodier
BOY WITH AIR GUN   Jason Cunliffe
HOSPITAL PATIENT   Dona Croll
NOSEBLEED POLICEMAN   Andrew Schofield
POLICE DRIVER   Jimmy Culshaw

WITH THE PARTICIPATION OF
GRAEME SOUNESS AND SAMMY LEE

1. Interior. Folly.

Yosser and his three children are exploring the inside of a Folly. We see the outside of the Folly. They look out and see the following events.

1a. Exterior. Lake. Evening.

The scene is a lake at evening time, in a Liverpool park. There are shadows on the ground and the sun is coming through the trees. Boats are being rowed on the lake. We see Yosser approaching the water's edge with his children. All four are fully clothed. A number of people sitting on the bank watch them as they march on towards the lake. They step right in and walk till they have to swim. The eldest boy and girl can swim well. The youngest has to hold on to Yosser as it gets deeper. Yosser treads water, then turns to the water's edge where the people have gathered. He whispers.

YOSSER. I'm Yosser Hughes.

His face remains expressionless. The two eldest are swimming. The youngest has disappeared. Yosser looks around.

YOSSER. Dustin. Dustin. Dustin!

As he turns, a boat goes slowly past him and the children. The boat is being rowed by a man with his back turned to us. But we see he is dressed in a surgeon's tunic and mask. Lying in the boat, in his pyjamas with a pillow behind his head, is George. He looks at Yosser as he goes past.

YOSSER. George, George, it's Yosser. Where's Dustin? George, where's Dustin? Dustin!

George shakes his head. As Yosser watches the boat going away, his eldest boy takes hold of him. Yosser looks away from George, bewildered and hurt. Puts his arms around his two clinging children and takes them under the water for the first time. We see the empty lake. Yosser and Jason, the eldest, re-emerge. Yosser looks around and cries out.

'Anne Marie, Anne Marie! Dustin!'

Another boat is approaching. We see Loggo and Chrissie. They are dressed like contestants at the Henley Regatta. Chrissie is the cox and Loggo is on the oars. They sweep past him, glance once at him in almost mechanical unison and then dismiss him.

YOSSER. Boys, boys, boys, it's me, Yosser. I'm losing my children, boys, boys.

No reply. The crowds around the edge of the lake wave and Yosser takes Jason down for the second time. We see them underwater. There is silence. A boat rows by. He surfaces alone. Yosser looks all round him. We see, from his point of view, Maureen, his wife, in another rowing boat, approaching him. A man who will later be identified as Moey is rowing the boat. Maureen is dressed to overkill. The boat gets closer to Yoseer than all the others, and just misses him, but Maureen doesn't even look at him. Yosser shouts to her as the boat is parallel with him.

YOSSER. Maureen, Maureen . . . Maureen! It's me, Maureen. I've lost them, Maureen, it's me!

The waves from the boat splash over him as it goes away. And Yosser closes his eyes. He pushes up in the water and then hurtles down. We see him alone underwater. Into blackness.

2. Interior. Yosser's bedroom. Night.

Blackness. Then in the darkness, we hear Yosser mumbling, then shouting.

YOSSER. No . . . no . . . No! Oh no.

He is breathing heavily. A light goes on. We are in Yosser's bedroom. His hand still on the dangling flex for the light switch, he looks over and sees his children all fast asleep in the double bed. He sits up in bed still breathing hard.

3. Interior. Department of Employment. Main Hall. Day.

The counter-clerk is behind a grille. Yosser is leaning forward, staring straight ahead through the wire. He is framed by his children. They all look desperately tired and uncared for. Yosser appears to be in a mood of manic calm as he stares at the clerk.

CLERK. ... Mr Hughes. Mr Hughes... I can't help you if you don't tell me what you want. I have your details here, but if you won't speak to me ... is it ... is it your children, their mother ... it's not my job to ... but you don't seem to be drawing your full entitled ... benefits ... would you like to talk to anyone else about your ... position? Mr Hughes? Mr Hughes? ... Mr Hughes.

Quietly.

Mr Hughes, my wife is a social worker, I can ask her to call in and see ...

Yosser nods his head once and mumbles.

CLERK. What? Pardon, Mr Hughes. Did you say something then?

Yosser leans forward, with apparent menace. But then he speaks.

YOSSER. Goodbye.

4. Interior. Malloy's Plant Shed. Day.

We see Malloy, the builder established in earlier episodes. He is in his plant shed, fussing over and setting up a 30-cwt power hammer. We hear Yosser from the doorway.

YOSSER. Gizza job, go –

Malloy turns and sees Yosser and the children in the doorway.

YOSSER. Oh. Right. Fair enough. (*He turns away, then turns back.*) Go on though, I can do that, I know how to work them.

Malloy doesn't look at Yosser. He speaks flatly.

MALLOY. I haven't got any jobs. There are no jobs here anymore. For one reason or another. I laid off fourteen men yesterday. I grew up with some of them.

Malloy tests the power hammer. It comes crashing down violently.

MALLOY. Good fun hey?

YOSSER. Gizza job.

*But Yosser is already walking away with his children. Malloy
watches him go, then walks towards the door and locks it. He walks
back and kneels down, almost sideways, beneath the power hammer so
that his head is directly beneath the hammer. Malloy lies still. Then
he reaches around the side towards the button to operate the hammer.*

4a. Exterior. Outside Plant Shed. Day.

*We see Yosser and his children walking away from the Plant Shed. We hear the
echoing bang from the power hammer. Yosser's children look around. Yosser
keeps going. He speaks flatly.*

YOSSER. I could have done that . . .

4b. Exterior. Playing field. Day.

*Yosser is on a school playing fields with his children. He is following a solitary
man who is marking the touchline for a football pitch. The man has already
heard enough.*

YOSSER. . . . Gizza job, go on, gizzit . . . gizza go, go on. I
could do that. You only have to walk straight. I can walk
straight, go on, gizza job, go on, gizza go.

*The man does a right-angle turn at the corner of the ptich, and heads
towards the goalposts. He has gone faster and faster to try and get
away. He doesn't look back. Yosser doesn't make the turn with him
but keeps walking straight.*

YOSSER. . . . I can put the nets up as well . . .

His children run to join him.

6.   Exterior. Playground. Day.

It is daytime, we are in a Liverpool park. There is a play area with swings, a

*slide, monkey ladders, and a merry-go-round. Underneath a tree sit
Yosser and his children, watching. Dustin is playing with a stick. He
seems happy.*

DUSTIN. What are we going to do?

ANNE MARIE. Dunno.

> *She leans on Yosser. We see what they are watching: a family, a
> father and mother and three children in the play area. They are
> enjoying themselves. The mother and father are pushing the children
> on the swings. Yosser and his children watch. Then the mother gets
> on the slide and the father catches her and picks her up. They are
> laughing happily, while Yosser and the children continue to watch. As
> a solitary magpie takes off from the ground, we see Yosser turn
> sharply away from the scene and butt the tree as hard as he can. Four
> times. The children keep facing out, and the magpie flies off.*

6. Interior. Flat (living room). Day.

*Maureen is peeping out and down through closed curtains of a high-rise flat.
Moey, the man she is living with, is in the hall tuning his drums. She crosses,
sits on the sofa and calls 'Moey' then gets up and looks out of window.*

MAUREEN. Moey. Do something, Moey!

MOEY. Yeah alright. (*He does nothing and carries on tuning.*)

MAUREEN. . . . Well, what're you going to do then?

> *Moey comes to the door.*

MOEY. Have a heart attack.

> *We see Moey front on. He has been beaten black and blue.*

MOEY. Listen Maureen, it's been very nice and all that, but I'm
not a brave man and I don't want to live with you anymore.
Or to be more specific, I don't want you to live with me
anymore.

> *Maureen gets up and rushes to Moey. He grabs her.*

Maureen I want you to go. Now.

*She breaks away. Moey goes back into the hall, where she joins him.
When he starts playing the bongos, she then crosses into the bedroom
muttering*

Bastard, Bastard.

Moey cleans the bongos.

MAUREEN. But what about him?

MOEY. (*Flatly.*) Go out the back way. Dig a tunnel. Get airlifted
out, wait till it goes dark. But go. (*He crosses into the bedroom to
collect his costume then goes out again.*)

MAUREEN. But where am I going to go?

There is a long pause.

MOEY. South America?

She gestures two fingers at Moey and the world in general.

7. Exterior. The back of the flats. Night.

*Maureen, struggling with the weight of two suitcases, slips out of the
block of high-rise flats. As she approaches a recess near a lamp post, out
of the shadows of the recess and into the light comes Yosser, in a surge
of movement.*

MAUREEN. For Christ's sake leave me alone you bastard, I don't
want you anymore.

*She squeals and tries to knee him. He pushes her against the lamp-
post as she drops her suitcases on the ground. Yosser takes hold of
Maureen by the hair and leans back as if to butt her, but as he
brings his head forward with force, he moves her head sideways and
deliberately butts the lamp post. It obviously hurts. He moves her head
back into place in front of the lamp-post. We see Yosser's children
peering out of the recess.*

YOSSER. Come home. Please.

*He lets go of her hair and smiles. She laughs out loud. But it is
half-laugh, half-sob. He looks at her for a second or so, and as she*

stands there, he walks off, followed as always by his children, in and out of the the pools of light thrown by the street-lamps. We just hear his two younger children speak, totally without pathos, as they walk at either side of Yosser, each holding his hand.

ANNE MARIE. She used to be our mummy.

DUSTIN. I know.

In the distance Maureen starts to collect up her things.

8. Exterior. Yosser's house. Day.

There is a man knocking at Yosser's door. He turns to see Yosser and his three children approaching. Yosser, carrying a Tesco bag, and apparently in a hurry ignores him, opens the door and goes inside with the children. As this happens, the man speaks.

SCHOOL ATTENDANCE OFFICER. Mr Hughes? Mr Hughes, my name's Watkins, I'm the schools' attendance officer for the area. The headmistress informs me that your children have not been attending of late—

The door closes.

Mr Hughes . . .

Knocks on the door again. But there is no reply. Mr Watkins puts an official-looking envelope through the letterbox. As he turns away, the envelope comes flying out again but he does not see it and carries on walking away.

9. Interior. Yosser's kitchen and back kitchen. Day.

The kitchen is in a fine mess, with black bin bags overflowing and left by the back door, plates piled high in the sink, and everything in, on, or around the cooker blackened and burnt. A patch on the wall above the cooker looks as though it has caught fire. In one corner, several kittens and a cat are playing. Yosser is at the cooker murdering a pan of fish fingers. Burning toast sends smoke signals from the grill. Yosser is doing – and saying – everything at a frenetic pace. The three children are waiting at the table in the back kitchen. The eldest is laying the table. The other two are playing with the kittens.

YOSSER. You wanna dinner – you can have a dinner, I can cook, course I can cook, sod the chippy, leave it to me.

He throws the black and dead toast out from under the grill. It lands somewhere near a black bin bag. He starts again.

YOSSER. Never let it be said, even though they might say it. I can manage, no sweat, I can cook, course I can cook, who says I can't.

He turns the flame under the fish fingers even higher then swings round towards his children.

Won't be long now.

The children wait patiently while we hear sounds of disaster coming from the kitchen.

10.   Exterior. Chip shop. Day.

We cut to Yosser coming glumly out of a chip shop with a large bag of chips in his hands. The children are in attendance. He starts to walk away. The children run after him.

11.Exterior/Interior. Front door of Yosser's house. Day.

The door-knocker is rapped loudly. Inside the hall it is dark, but we see Yosser's eldest boy, Jason, walk to the front door in his pyjamas. He opens the door. We see a health visitor facing him. She is a lady of brisk, pleasant, matronly authority.

HEALTH VISITOR. Now you'll be Jason, won't you? there's a good boy, I've just come to have a few words with your father.

12.   Interior. Hall/Living room. Day.

The Health Visitor walks straight past the boy and into the small hallway.

Meanwhile, at the top of the stairs, the two youngest children are peeping around the corner of the bannisters but they dart back as she looks. She walks into the living room and has a good look round. Jason follows her to the door.

HEALTH VISITOR. Is your Dad still in bed?

Jason nods, and she says the next line to herself as she writes in her file.

Oh well, it is only ten to twelve.

She closes her file.

You don't mind if I wash my hands do you, dear?

As she marches off to the kitchen without waiting for a reply – or expecting one – the child has no option. We hear him hurry out of the living room and up the stairs.

13. Interior. Back kitchen. Day.

She enters the back kitchen, and as she does so we follow her and see her view of the debris. Despite the state of it she does not flicker, but simply writes some more in her file. Even after opening a cupboard she does not wash her hands. Finally she turns around as we see Yosser in a shirt and underpants arrive at the kitchen door. His children again, are behind him. Yosser whispers.

YOSSER. I know what you've come for. Wash your hands, my arsehole.

14. Interior. Back kitchen. Day.

Yosser is on his hands and knees in the back kitchen, scrubbing furiously at the floor. The bin bags have gone and the sink is empty. The cooker and work surfaces look a great deal cleaner. He appears to be talking to himself.

YOSSER. Well alright. So that's the game, yeah well, yeah yeah.

Laughs.

Okay right, they're not going to get me like that . . . and . . . we're

going out tonight . . . I'm taking you out tonight . . . you'll see us
there, me and Graeme. I'll make sure of that. They're not going to
make me look small, not in front of you . . . it's advertised and
I'm going . . . we all are . . .

15. Interior. Pub. Night.

*We are in the lounge of a public house where two models are moving a display of
flowers. It is obviously a charity do. The pub manager calls for quiet.*

'Order please'.

*We see Graeme Souness and Sammy Lee, both men immaculately dressed and
groomed, surrounded by 'well wishers'. The pub manager is between them. Lee
and Souness are about to push over a huge, high pillar of pennies on a table in
front of a crowd of photographers. Everyone is smiling and a roar goes up as the
money scatters. As the audience cheer and applaud, the girls collect up the
money and the media men take photos. Eventually the atmosphere settles
down and people move away. There is standard pub-type piped music in
the background throughout this scene. After signing a few autographs, Lee
goes through the remnants of the crowd, followed by Souness, towards a
table set out for them in a discreet corner. The manager's wife is
already waiting there. They sit down. The manager takes a bottle out of
a champagne bucket on the table and opens it. The cork pops. The
manager's wife pours it. As we look on, Yosser goes past us towards the
table. The manager is already twitching as Yosser goes to sit between
the two footballers. There is not very much space. The manager is about
to say something, when he looks out and sees something else that upsets
him. Yosser turns to Lee.*

YOSSER. Excuse me.

*Footballers are used to head-bangers and Lee wryly gives him space.
The pub manager finally speaks.*

PUB MANAGER. Ah-hey Yosser, no kids allowed, know what I
mean.

*He points towards where the children are. Yosser stares malignantly at
him.*

MANAGER. Well just this once, hey. Just for a few minutes.

*Then nobody says anything. The footballers sip at the drink. Yosser
turns slightly and looks at Souness. Souness looks at him, looks away
and then has to look again.*

YOSSER. You're Graeme Souness. Aren't you?

SOUNESS. Yes.

YOSSER. You're famous.

SOUNESS. Well . . .

YOSSER. I'm Yosser Hughes. *(As if this explains everything.)*

SOUNESS. Pleased to meet you.

Yosser leans towards him, as if about to disclose a secret.

YOSSER. . . . You look like me . . .

SOUNESS. Oh aye.

Yosser leans nearer still.

YOSSER. Magnum as well.

SOUNESS. Pardon?

YOSSER. Magnum. A detective. He used to be on the
television. An American.

SOUNESS. Oh Aye.

*Sammy Lee and the pub manager look on a bit bemused. Yosser
drags a scrap of paper from his pocket. Sammy Lee looks at the two
of them occasionally.*

YOSSER. Sign this, for us will y' Graeme?

SOUNESS. Sure.

He takes hold of the paper, and gets a pen out.

Who's it for?

He looks at the kids.

YOSSER. Me.

The kids smile.

SOUNESS. Erm . . .

YOSSER. Yosser Hughes.

His children look on. In an attempt to deflate the tension, Souness writes several words on the paper, then gives it back to Yosser who reads it.

YOSSER. 'To Yosser Hughes, better looking by far, best wishes, Graeme Souness.'

Yosser Hughes looks carefully at Souness, who shows no sign of irony.

YOSSER. Good that. Graeme.

Yosser looks away, past the camera, towards where his children and the other drinkers are. He is well pleased. Then he sits there, just facing out. There is a moment of terrible silence with all five facing out. The manager finally stands first, then his wife, quickly followed by both footballers. Quietly, with as little insult as possible, they begin to leave. Without looking at Yosser, Souness moves the champagne in front of him and then his own empty glass. They all walk away. We leave Yosser sitting there. He pours the champagne into a glass but doesn't drink it. He looks instead at the autograph in his hand, looks up and nods his head. Then he whispers the words to himself:

YOSSER. I could have been a footballer . . . but I had a paper round.

16.   Exterior. Yosser's house. Day.

A man from the Electricity Board is knocking on Yosser's front door. Yosser opens the door and looks down from his front step.

ELECTRICIAN. Manweb. I've come to turn off your power.

YOSSER. Have y' got a good dentist?

ELECTRICIAN. Ah come on, there's no need to threaten me, just close the door, that'll do me. All I have to do then is say I couldn't gain entry, and you've got two weeks grace.

No answer.

Y' don't have to close the door if y' don't want. I'll lie about it.

Yosser moves off the step.

I hate the job y' know. I don't want to disconnect people.

The electrician backs away towards his van. He coughs loud and false.

I've been off sick, they put me on this when I came back, I didn't ask for it . . . Look at me, I'm not that sort of person.

He gets to the van, and opens the door.

But I tell you what though pal, if y' don't pay up, it gets nasty y' know. They bring men in. I'm just warning y', that's all.

As the van goes off, we see Yosser standing a yard or two from his front door staring out. Two more men approach, one of them a rent collector, the other, with a briefcase attached to his left wrist, his minder. Yosser stares at him.

RENTMAN. *(Almost in passing.)* Morning Yosser, anything down for me? *(Nothing.)* Not even a gesture of goodwill? *(Still nothing).* Fair enough, but a friendly warning. If y' don't pay y' rent, well, y' won't have any rent to pay, if y' know what I mean. *(Still nothing.)* Don't say I didn't tell y'.

As the two men start to go off, Yosser takes hold of the minder's left arm. The minder looks down at Yosser's hand.

YOSSER. . . . Gizza job, go on, gizzit. I could do that. I can carry things. I've had practice.

The minder walks off. Yosser looks out.

17. Exterior. Yosser's house. Day.

A truck is parked up on the corner nearest Yosser's house. Maureen is sitting in the cab with two men. Yosser and his children leave the house and walk off. The children follow him, away from the truck. When Yosser momentarily turns round, Maureen and the two men lean back. She then looks out and indicates that they should approach the house. The truck moves up the road.

18.   Exterior. Yosser's house. Day.

Two men load the personal possessions into the back of the van.

19.   Interior. Yosser's living room. Day.

The armchairs have already gone and the room is beginning to look bare. Especially as there wasn't that much anyway. Maureen is pacing the floor, quietly measuring the carpet. She glances briefly at some letters on the mantelpiece, all of them formal. When the men return, one of them picks up a music centre.

MAUREEN. No, don't take that, it isn't paid for yet. There's a washing-machine and the fridge out there, but you can forget the cooker, it's destroyed . . .

The removal man picks up the coffee table while the other one goes into the back kitchen and starts to move the washing-machine. We see Maureen look at a photograph of the children on the mantelpiece. She looks at it for a bit, expressionless. But then she puts it face down before throwing her house keys on the mantelpiece.

20.   Interior. Yosser's living room. Day.

Now that the furniture has been removed the boys have enough room to play football in the living room. That is just what they are doing. Meanwhile, the girl is drawing on the wall. Two people, a frail, bird-like woman, and a young man knock on the open front door.

MORGAN. Hello.

They walk in, through the hall, and into the living room. The carpet has gone as well. All that's left is bare boards and a music centre. We see Yosser leaning his head on the wall above the mantelpiece, above where the gas fire used to be. He has hold of Maureen's house keys limply.

MORGAN. (*To the kids.*) Hello lads, give us a kick, then, go on.

Morgan knocks on the living-room door.

MORGAN. Mr Hughes? Sorry, the door was open, er, we're from the Social Services, my name's Morgan –

As he speaks, the woman squats down in front of Yosser's daughter and smiles warmly.

VERONICA. Hello. I'm Veronica.

Yosser remains still and speaks quietly without looking round as if he has not heard the introductions being made.

YOSSER. I'm Yosser Hughes . . . This is my house, get out of my house.

When the children gather round Yosser, Veronica crosses over to them and bends again.

VERONICA. And what's your name?

The children do not answer.

YOSSER. They're my children, they're staying with me. I'm Yosser Hughes.

He stays where he is as the social workers exchange glances and look at the state of the room.

21. Exterior. Pier Head. Day.

We see Yosser, and then his children, against a background of the Liver Buildings at the Pier-Head. He is amid the winos and derelicts on the benches, staring out, apparently unaware of everything around himself. His children are leaning over the railings, and they too reflect his vacancy. They are all becoming progressively more rough and dirty. Just above the noise of the crowd, we hear Yosser mumbling totally to himself at first.

YOSSER. It's alright, it's alright, it's alright though . . . I'm Yosser Hughes 'better looking by far'. *(He grins.)* Everybody knows that. Everybody knows me. Everybody notices me. *(He turns to the wino sitting beside him.)* You've noticed me, haven't you?

Yosser takes hold of the wino's arm as the wino lifts a bottle in a brown paper bag up to his lips. The wino is Scottish, in his fifties.

WINO. Leave my disinfectant alone.

YOSSER. I like to be noticed. Have you . . . noticed that?

Yosser laughs at the lunacy of what he is saying. But he puts his hand back on the man's arm.

WINO. I won't tell you again.

YOSSER. Everywhere I go I get noticed. That's me.

Yosser keeps smiling and won't let go of his arm. The wino makes a half-hearted attempt to rid himself of Yosser. Then he stops.

WINO. Are you . . . are you after my body?

Yosser seems to weigh the question up.

YOSSER. No. Everybody knows that. Everybody knows me. Graeme Souness knows me.

WINO. Souness, Aye.

YOSSER. I'm Yosser Hughes.

WINO. Listen, come on, listen to me. I want to tell you something.

YOSSER. I know. I'm Yosser Hughes.

WINO. No listen, Jimmy.

YOSSER. Yosser.

WINO. Yosser, they water this stuff down you know. They do. In the factory. I know, I have contacts.

He taps his nose. He drinks from the bottle in the bag.

It's cold in this city, even in the summer. Eventually I shall migrate south for the winter . . . You can have my body if you want, I'm past caring.

Again we see the children leaning over the railings watching the ferries. Jason walks up and down. Yosser is still staring out front.

YOSSER. When I was little . . . when I was. There was so much to look forward to. Then. In the . . . in the fifties.

When I was little. I built sandcastles.

Anne Marie comes to sit next to Yosser. When Yosser puts his arm around his daughter, the wino looks around slowly and absurdly to see if anyone is watching.

WINO. Hey wait a minute.

The wino then pulls out from a pocket inside his overcoat a packet of Babycham chocolate liqueurs and holds them up to Yosser. Except that Yosser isn't looking.

WINO. Thirty pence. Heh? Thirty. *(He looks at Yosser.)* Hey. You. For the little lady in your life.

Yosser turns towards the wino, and takes hold of him by the lapels.

YOSSER. *I built sandcastles.* And . . . I sometimes think that's all I've ever done.

Anne Marie has joined the other two at the railings again and they all three stare out.

22.   Interior. Interview Room. Day.

We see Maureen in close up. She is being interviewed. The whole delivery is documentary, perhaps almost like 'World in Action'. She is smoking heavily.

MAUREEN. He hit me. A lot. All the time as a matter of fact. That's why I went out. But when I came back in, he'd hit me again. So I started not coming in at all. Look. I know it sounds awful, but it was him. He made me.

There is a heavy pause. She feels that this isn't enough.

He was doing all kinds of daft things. He got this job in Saudi. And he made us move to this stupid big house. I don't know who he was trying to impress, but we couldn't possibly afford it. Then he lost his job. That really did send him down. And then, when they came knockin', it was then he started hittin' the kids. He did. He'd take it out on them. And he'd lock them in their bedroom at night. Without food . . . I couldn't cope in the end. I had a sort of breakdown and I couldn't bear to be near him anymore. Or the kids. Because of what he'd done to me. And them. They didn't seem like mine anymore. That's why I don't want them now. They remind me. I'm sorry but I couldn't cope . . .

She leans forward.

If it's any help to you, I don't think they're his neither. I shouldn't say this, but there's a good chance they're not. When we were married I had this sort of friend . . . Well. It was the only thing that kept me sane . . . You only have to look at them really. We've both got black hair, and the kids are blond . . . My friend was blond . . . he was a German sea-captain. You can use that, if you want. I'm going away anyway, he won't find me where I'm going . . . He wasn't very good, you know, He wasn't very good at anything. That was part of the trouble. He thought he was. And he always thought he was going to be somebody.

She laughs.

And really he was nothing.

She stares out.

Is that enough?

We fade to black.

23. Exterior. Private house. Day.

We fade up from black to see Yosser carrying a plastic bag of kittens, and each child carrying a kitten. Nearby, some builders are working in front of a house. We see George Malone stagger and fall on to a pile of sand. Yosser and the kids are trying and failing to sell kittens to the lady of the house. They leave with the owner following them into the drive and looking after them. Yosser and the kids approach the builders.

YOSSER. Wanna buy . . .

He and we see George, holding a spade, lying on a tip of sand, alongside of which are several bags of cement and bricks in piles of four hundred. George is dressed in a donkey jacket, pyjama bottoms and a pair of slippers. A brickie and his mate stare at George, unbelieving.

YOSSER. George? George.

Yosser drops the bag he is carrying. As the scene continues, several kittens crawl out of the bag and make their escape.

YOSSER. George, George!

Yosser picks George up off the sand.

24. Exterior. Hospital. Day.

We see Yosser approaching the entrance gates to a hospital. We should not see for some time that Yosser is pushing George in a wheelbarrow. His children are straggling behind. It is, at first, as if Yosser is talking to himself.

YOSSER. Y'see George, it's the pressure. They're all after me. But if I was someone famous or y'know important, they wouldn't be. Am I right? If I was someone, they'd leave me alone. Y' don't stand a chance when y'no one, you've always said that an' you're spot on. They want my kids now. They've got everything else, now they want them as well. Listen, George, I can talk to you, George, you know everything, you're a great help to me . . . I'm not boring you, am I, George? George? Y' see, the thing is, I was alright when I was little, I was the king of the castle, but now I wet meself all the time . . . George, George, what am I going to do? . . . What George?

George is plainly unconscious as Yosser takes him into the interior of the hospital.

25. Interior. Catholic Church. Day.

We see the interior light of a Roman Catholic church. It is almost empty, dimly lit and old-fashioned, full of candles, flowers, leaded

windows and statues of the Virgin. Along one wall is a row of statues,
each one with a plaque underneath it indicating one of the Stations of the
Cross.

26. Interior. Confessional box. Day

A priest in his mid-thirties is sitting on his side of the Confessional in
an old armchair. On the wall facing him is a square wood-framed grille
with small curtains across it to protect the identity of the guilty. On the
small table by his chair there are two books, 'A Book of Irish Wit and
Humour' and 'For Whom the Bell Tolls'. Alongside the books are a
packet of Bassett's Jelly Babies and an empty tea cup and saucer. The
priest has his eyes closed. As the door to the Confessional opens, the
priest opens his eyes and we hear someone shuffle in on the sinner's side
of the box. A second's silence, then, instead of the expected sound of the
door closing again, more feet are heard. He hears the giggling of a group
of children as they come in.

PRIEST. . . . Yes? . . . Hello?

The door finally closes. Someone kneels down. The priest is slightly
unnerved by the giggles and the knowledge that there is a whole group
of people out there.

PRIEST. . . . One at a time please. This isn't a spectator sport!

He laughs a little but gets no reaction.

PRIEST. Would you like to begin your confession?

The giggling continues. Then the children tell each other to shut
up, and settle down.

PRIEST. Excuse me, excuse me. Would you like to start your
confession now? Thank you.

We can hear someone breathing, heavily but non-sexual. The priest
takes hold of the curtains and draws them back fast. Yosser is framed
by the square grille, with the light in his side of the box directly
above him. He is staring out, facing the priest, wild-eyed, both
frightened and frightening. Behind him, standing up by the door are
his children. The priest pulls the curtain back across the grille.

PRIEST. Oh! I'm sorry. I . . . vandals, you know. You can never be too . . . I shouldn't really hear your confession in the presence of anyone else, but the – er – children . . . your children? They're . . . if it's not a confession of any . . . consequence . . . er, turmoil.

There is still no answer, but the noise of the breathing increases. We hear a sobbing noise for a second.

You . . . you do require confession, my son?

Yosser gives no answer, but continues sobbing as the priest, who by now is genuinely aware of the man's condition, speaks.

Do you want to talk to me, just . . . talk? You tell me . . .

But still there is no answer.

Whatever you want, you tell me. That's what I'm here for. Through me, you can talk to . . .

The priest looks up at the heavens and begins to point as he talks, but decides against bringing God into this.

whoever might want to be listening. As it were. We are the guardians of the spirit, my son. Some kind of help in times of need . . .

Yosser finally stumbles out some words as we see the children quiet and listening.

YOSSER. Father, father . . . I'm . . . I'm . . .

PRIEST. Yes?

YOSSER. I'm . . . I'm Yosser Hughes.

PRIEST. There's no need to tell me your . . .

YOSSER. I'm desperate, father. Des . . . perate.

PRIEST. It can be a desperate world at times, Mr Hugh—

YOSSER. Yosser Hughes.

PRIEST. It can be a desperate world at times yosserhughes. Tell me, if it makes it any easier . . .

Yosser is still sobbing. The priest goes again to take hold of the curtain, but stops. He talks over Yosser's sobs.

PRIEST. A trouble shared in a place of peace, my son. A haven.
I'm Father Thomas. 'Doubting' for short!

He opens the curtain again as he repeats the 'joke'.

Doubting Thomas.

*Yosser has his head resting against the grille, his hands clasped
together, knuckles white.*

Daniel Thomas. I'm here to help you, yosserhughes.
Daniel. Don't worry about the 'father'.

YOSSER. I'm desperate, father.

Yosser looks up at the priest, then closes his eyes.

PRIEST. Call me Dan. Dan.

YOSSER. I'm desperate. Dan.

*Yosser looks up at the priest again. There is a fraction of a manic
glance and he tries to laugh. Then he stops instantly. He seems to be
screaming silently as he leans back and then brings his head forward
to butt the wooden frame surrounding the wire grille. The crucifix
above drops down and hits him as he then butts and butts and butts
the wire grille.*

27.   Interior. Hospital Foyer.

*We see the entrance of a busy hospital. Yosser and his three
children walk in through the front door and go up the stairs.*

**28.   Interior. Doctor's Consulting Room, Psychiatric Unit.
Day.**

*The Consulting Room is a bare white room with a waiting area/hall
outside. The furniture consists of a desk, a doctor's examining couch in
one corner, and two chairs. A lady in her late thirties is facing across the
desk. Her face is severe.*

ANNE MARIE. I wanna go home, why can't we go home?

DOCTOR. I will not talk to you with your children present. It is as simple as that.

Yosser is sitting down in the doctor's room, with his children, whining and tetchy, in front of him, where he can see them, and in between him and the doctor. Sometimes he talks sanely and logically. Sometimes not.

YOSSER. Father Thomas did.

DOCTOR. I am not a priest, Mr Hughes.

YOSSER. Just as well really. The Catholic Church has enough problems without women.

He smiles.

YOSSER. Doctor.

Anne Marie whines throughout.

DOCTOR. Take your children into the waiting area and I will talk to you. About your children for a start.

YOSSER. No. They're staying where I can see them. It's a trick. They won't be there when I come out.

DOCTOR. Oh come on.

YOSSER. It's true.

DOCTOR. Ah yes, the conspiracy theory. The whole world is against you.

YOSSER. That's not true. But you don't like me, do you?

DOCTOR. That's neither here nor—

YOSSER. Nobody likes me.

DOCTOR. Take your children outside and we can talk.

YOSSER. No chance.

DOCTOR. Leave the door open so that you can see them.

YOSSER. Someone'll snatch them. Someone'll lock the door from the outside and they'll be gone. And when that happens, you're dead.

DOCTOR. (*Gently.*) Please take your children outside, and if you won't do that, please take yourself outside.

YOSSER. (*Peering between his children.*) I'm Yosser Hughes.

DOCTOR. Mr Hughes, you are putting yourself, your children and the parental custody of your children at risk by your behaviour.

YOSSER. Don't talk like that in front of my children.

The frenzied pace drops for a space and Yosser leans forward.

YOSSER. Look, I only came here 'cos I had to. I'm not cracked. There's nothing wrong with me. I'm Yosser Hughes.

DOCTOR. Goodbye, Mr Hughes.

She goes to write in the case book she has in front of her. Yosser stands up, goes to the door with his children, opens the door and looks out into the waiting area. Then he moves a few yards out of the office with the children and places them where he can see them. They stand there, not moving. Yosser backs in to the Doctor, and stands at the far corner of her desk, not looking at her at all, staring out of the door.

YOSSER. Why? Why?

DOCTOR. Mr Hughes you have to face facts. Your wife does not want to see you anymore.

YOSSER. But why? Why?

DOCTOR. Surely the events speak for themselves.

YOSSER. They haven't talked to me.

DOCTOR. Possibly because you won't listen.

The doctor becomes more gentle.

DOCTOR. This is getting us nowhere. Please either sit down and discuss this matter or . . . leave the room.

Yosser promptly sits on the side of her desk, his back to her, still looking out towards the waiting area.

DOCTOR. You cannot condone what you have done, Mr Hughes. You have attacked your wife. And her . . . associates. Physically attacked them.

YOSSER. I was provoked.

DOCTOR. Physically?

YOSSER. Mental's worse.

Yosser looks at her for the first time since he came back into the room. And leans on her desk.

You'd support that argument wouldn't you?

Grins and then stops.

You know why you're called a shrink, don't y'? 'Cos y' shrink people – that's what y' tryin' to do to me – but y' won't an' y' know why – 'cos I'm Yosser Hughes, y' won't shrink me. She tried that, she used to shrink everythin'. One wash and there it was – fit for a midget.

He laughs and stops.

I want her back.

He is still looking at her.

DOCTOR. . . . But she isn't coming back.

YOSSER. I don't really want her back.

DOCTOR. Well then.

YOSSER. I just want her there.

DOCTOR. *(Gently.)* I feel just like that sometimes. About my three-piece suite.

Yosser sits down at last.

YOSSER. She's not coming back, is she?

DOCTOR. I don't think so.

YOSSER. That's alright. All she ever did was frig off. She never cooked for me or nothin'. She didn't love me. She didn't love the kids. I know you want to talk to me about the kids. I want to keep the kids.

No answer.

I want to keep the kids.

He looks away towards the kids but they aren't there in the doorway. He virtually leaps off the chair towards the chair and goes flying out of the door in total panic. He runs up and down the waiting area outside her office in mounting panic.

29.   Interior. Lifts at Day Clinic. Day.

He runs down the corridor, and then sees the three children just a couple of yards away at the lift doorway. The eldest has his hand near the button. The lift door is open. Yosser dives for the lift, expecting to see the kidnappers in there. But he cannot see into the lift until he enters it at a great pace, ready to kill. There is nobody there at all. He looks at his children with desperate anxiety, and goes down on his knees. The doctor follows down the corridor. The eldest presses the lift button just as the doors are beginning to close on Yosser. He tries to get up off his knees to the door.

JASON. We were just . . .

And as the doors close, the doctor joins Yosser's children outside the lift.

YOSSER. Let me out. It's a trap. Anne Marie, stay there.
Dustin, don't go with them. Stay there, Jason.

DOCTOR. Mr Hughes. It's alright, they're with me.

Yosser presses a button. We hear Yosser going away.

YOSSER. Stay there, stay there . . .

The lift starts to go to the ground floor. The lift doors open on to the ground floor foyer, then close again. The doctor kneels down on her haunches to Yosser's children. We see that they appear tired, withdrawn and distant, as well as dirt-stained. Only their eyes, constantly looking around, give any sign of emotion or nervousness.

DOCTOR. Are you alright?

They all nod.

Are you sure?

We hear the sound of Yosser butting the instrument panel as the lift returns and the doors open again. At an angle, we see Yosser at the side of the lift interior. Butting the instrument panel. He is crying.

YOSSER. Don't touch them, leave them alone . . . Don't touch 'em.

And the doors close again on him. He makes no attempt to stop them from shutting.

30. Interior. Yosser's bedroom. Night.

The children are in their pyjamas on the double bed. Anne Marie is singing 'All Things Bright And Beautiful' the boys are reading magazines and drawing.

JASON. Shut up, Anne Marie.

She whispers the words, gradually getting back to singing it again. Yosser comes through the doorway looks in on his children, ruffles Dustin's hair and sits down on the single bed.

YOSSER. . . . When you were born y'know, when you were born . . . I mean, when you were born. Then it was . . . it was . . . I was alright then. Without me you . . . But I didn't know then. You don't know. You never know. You think you do, but you don't.

Inevitably they are not listening to him. Even if they were, they wouldn't understand what he is talking about. Yosser goes to them and

*lies down on the double bed. The youngest lies down beside him and
cuddles his father.*

31. Interior. Yosser's living room. Day.

*The two people from the Social Services Department are back again,
gently, patiently trying to explain it all to Yosser.*

MORGAN. Mr Hughes, I'm sorry but we do have authority
under the Children's Act and Young People's Act of 1969 to
remove your children regardless of your permission or not.

VERONICA. We only want them to receive proper care, Mr
Hughes.

*We see Yosser from a few yards away. He lifts the small bird-like
social worker up by her coat, revealing his unacceptable side, with
trumps. The lady is dangling between Yosser and the other social
worker who is behind her.*

YOSSER. Care? Care? What do you care. You can't care for
them like I care for them.

*Yosser drops the lady social worker and pushes her away on to the
male social worker's feet. When the back of her head hits the male
social worker in the face, he doesn't know whether to limp or have a
nosebleed.*

VERONICA. (*To Morgan.*) Are you alright?

YOSSER. I'm sorry. No, sorry. Sorry.

He touches her lapels.

. . . You'd better go away.

VERONICA. Calm down, Mr Hughes.

YOSSER. No, you better had. I'm caring for them. There's no
need for a place of safety. They've got me . . .

He pursues them down the hall.

YOSSER. . . . 'Cos listen, you can summons me to see a

magistrate till life everlasting. I'm not goin'. There's no one in need here. Listen, I'm telling you, and you'd better believe me, don't come back unless you bring an army.

Yosser is at the front door and Morgan and Veronica are running into the road. Yosser slams the door.

32.   Exterior. Yosser's house. Day.

The army Yosser was talking about has arrived and are waiting patiently, for the inevitable. The two social workers are knocking at the downstairs window of Yosser's house. One of them is waving a 'Place of Safety Order'. They call as they knock.

MORGAN. Mr Hughes.

VERONICA. Mr Hughes.

MORGAN. It's Morgan and Veronica from the Social Services, Mr Hughes.

VERONICA. Please come out, Mr Hughes.

MORGAN. Please, Mr Hughes, just a quick word.

VERONICA. Mr Hughes. If you'd just come to the door, Mr Hughes.

A third social worker knocks on the door and keeps knocking and knocking. A Social Services mini-bus is parked a little way down the road with three or four men inside. One of the social workers crosses over to a police car which is parked alongside it, full of policemen. A small crowd is gathering at the edges of the scene.

SOCIAL WORKER. We can handle this ourselves, we don't need you, we just need a bit more time.

We do not see Yosser or the children. Morgan and Veronica are still trying to raise Yosser, when they are joined by the driver of the police car. He has a large half-circle scar on his face.

SCARFACE POLICEMAN. You're new at this job, aren't y', love?

VERONICA. Yes, but I don't see what that's got to do with . . .

SCARFACE POLICEMAN. How old are you – sixteen, seventeen?

MORGAN. Hey now, just hold on pal.

SCARFACE POLICMAN. Leave it to me, alright? Otherwise we'll be here all day.

He begins to walk away.

Y' don't get anywhere bein' pleasant to shite.

He goes to the car and gets the other three policemen out.

Andy, you go by the front door, the rest of you round the back with me.

The social workers at the window resume knocking and calling and looking into the living room.

MOSS. Mr Hughes!

VERONICA. Mr Hughes!

MORGAN. I think it'd be better if you did come out now, Mr Hughes.

VERONICA. Mr Hughes!

As the three policemen run round the back, a policeman and dog get out of a police van and wait.

MORGAN. Mr Hughes, please, Mr Hughes!

They are knocking even more frantically.

33. Exterior/Interior. Back yard/back kitchen/living room. Day.

The policemen kick the back gate and smash the glass in the back door. They unbolt the door and they are in. Yosser appears from the shadowy light in the hall, and runs down the stairs, wielding a baseball bat. He confronts the policeman in the kitchen.

SCARFACE POLICEMAN. Put it down you bastard!

The three policemen now have their truncheons drawn. It is Cowboys and Indians time. Yosser takes one swing with the bat, but is hit from all sides. And hit and hit until he falls down. Yosser attempts to fight back but he doesn't stand a chance. Veronica and Morgan can only watch helplessly through the window. While Scarface watches with a smirk on his face.

34.   Exterior. Yosser's house. Day.

At the end of this beating, Veronica turns away from the window, and looks straight out, facing us with a shocked and sickened look on her face. Scarface walks from the living room into the hall followed by the other policemen. He is obviously well pleased with his day's work. Morgan and Veronica are on their way in.

SCARFACE POLICEMAN. They're all yours. They're under the bed upstairs.

VERONICA. Well, you bastard!

They go inside and up the stairs. Scarface grins happily at her, and then he and his companions walk back to the car, strutting big men. Until a single airgun shot rings out, and Scarface howls, holding his backside.

SCARFACE POLICEMAN. I've been shot, I've been shot!

Scarface and the other three policemen dive out of sight behind their cars. Now we see a boy in a first floor window with an airgun firing determinedly at them. They are trapped behind their cars as more shots are fired and more ducking follows.

We see the lad with the air gun being dragged out of his house by the policeman and bundled into the police car. We faintly hear his solitary protest.

SCAREFACE POLICEMAN. Come on.

BOY WITH AIR GUN. But I'm a hero . . .

SCARFACE. Shut up.

35.   Exterior. Yosser's house. Day.

We come back as Yosser's children are being brought down the stairs from the bedroom and out of the house. Morgan and a male social worker are carrying a boy each, and Veronica has hold of the daughter. All three children are screaming and resisting care. Wildly. We see Yosser lying still on the floor.

Dialogue throughout the scene

KIDS. No, no, no what about my dad? Dad! Put me down! Dad!

VERONICA. Your daddy is going to be alright, Anne Marie.

KIDS. No! No!

MORGAN. It's alright you're going to see your daddy soon, it's alright.

ANNE MARIE. Dad!

VERONICA. It's alright.

We focus on Veronica and Anne Marie. Veronica is carrying the girl, and holding her wrists to stop her from fighting. The girl stops struggling as they get to the mini van and stares at Veronica for a second. Veronica smiles at her reassuringly. The smile is returned. Happiness is restored. Then Anne Marie butts her in the face. Veronica squeals.

VERONICA. Ooh you little . . .

Anne Marie looks well pleased.

36.   Interior. Yosser's living room. Day.

We pan around the empty living room on to Yosser who is sitting huddled in a corner, with four days' growth of beard. He is wearing his overcoat, and has two empty milk bottles at his side, as well as two packets of cornflakes, the remnants of a sliced loaf, a tub of margarine, an empty tin of spam, and a knife. He also has a black eye, the bruising well out and flourishing. We hold on him. He stares out. It is as if he has stared out for days, but then, as we hold, some animation comes into his face. He starts to nod his head slightly, as if he had reached a decision. He begins to struggle to his feet. A floorboard creaks.

37. Interior. Hospital. Day.

The woman psychiatrist is in her room with a black female patient who is smoking heavily.

DOCTOR. How many do you think you need?

HOSPITAL PATIENT. Well, four a day, but I need more on Sunda—

> *The doctor's door bursts open and Yosser enters as if he has just finished running a four-minute mile. He stands a few yards into the room, out of breath and shaking.*

YOSSER. Where are they – WHERE ARE THEY? I've been looking for them but I can't find them. I couldn't even find you. Where are they? You know, you must know, you put them away. You must know where they are. Where are they?

> *He turns and leans against the wall, head first, back turned. His pose has as much exhaustion in it as pleading.*

DOCTOR. Mr. Hughes, to be absolutely honest, in all truth . . .

YOSSER. Yeah, they all start like that and then they tell me lies. Where are they? I've been everywhere looking for them. I've been to Bellevale and Marsh Lane—

HOSPITAL PATIENT. (*Flatly.*) That's where mine are.

YOSSER. I've been to the Cenocle and Mount Pleasant—

HOSPITAL PATIENT. Excuse me—

YOSSER. I can't find them anywhere. Where are they?

HOSPITAL PATIENT. Excuse me, but this is my appointment. It took me three buses to get here, and you only get a quarter of an hour anyway.

DOCTOR. If you would just wait outside, Mr Hughes.

YOSSER. No!

He collapses on to the floor by the wall.

DOCTOR. Please.

PATIENT. This isn't fair, you know. And there's a queue.

DOCTOR. Please wait outside, Mr Hughes.

YOSSER. Put me away, hey?

He get up and crawls to lean on the edge of her desk, pleading, but with suppressed rage.

Send me away. Where are they? Let me be with them. WHERE ARE THEY? Let me be with them. Mm? Put me away too. Mm? I can be with them . . . I can be with them.

Yosser looks up at the doctor, puts his index finger up to his bottom lip, and flicks at his lip, making blubbering noises like a child. He tries to smile, but it descends quickly to tears, then to solid, pained weeping. His body shaking, near to convulsion, he huddles into the corner, hands over his head. The female patient watches him, becoming just ever so slightly alarmed. The doctor picks up her phone and begins dialling.

HOSPITAL PATIENT. What . . . what's he doing that for?

DOCTOR. Penance . . .

We leave on Yosser's huddled weeping.

38. Exterior. Yosser's house. Day.

Two men stack plywood against the railing outside Yosser's house, and then go to join a third man with an official-looking piece of paper who is leaning against a car. They wait until they, and we, see Yosser come slowly down the street and go into his house. The man with the paper goes to him.

EVICTION MAN. I'm sorry about this, sir, it's an eviction order, and we'd like as little fuss as possible please. For your own good.

YOSSER. Have it, go on, have it. May you always be . . .

Yosser goes inside the house as the eviction man gestures to the men, who go and start nailing the plywood across the windows.

39.   Exterior. Yosser's house. Day.

We see one of the men knocking the final plywood into place across a window. What little stuff was left in the house has been piled spreadeagled in the street. Yosser comes out of the front door and starts walking away past the furniture. He is holding limply at his side the photograph of his children that was on the mantelpiece. As he passes the men and the plywood, he has a last, desperate attempt.

YOSSER.   . . . I could do that . . .

As he goes, he takes the photograph from its frame, throws the frame on to the pile of furniture, and walks away clutching the photograph.

40.   Exterior. Williamson Square. Early morning.

It is the early hours of the morning. There is heavy rain. Apart from Yosser sitting on a bench, soaked, and looking like a tramp, Williamson Square is deserted. We see another figure approaching from Whitechapel. He sits down next to Yosser. It is the Scottish wino.

WINO. Lend me ten shillings. I need ten shillings for shoes. I'll get you a pair as well. I'll come back with them. *(He looks at Yosser for the first time.)* Don't I know you from somewhere?

YOSSER. I'm . . . I'm . . . I'm wet.

WINO. It's the climate son.

YOSSER. I wish I was dead.

WINO. It's this city, man. Naw, if I had decent shoes I'd
be awa'. F. Off, Vamoos (*Pause.*) I'm not sitting here much
longer, I can tell you. It's all wet. (*Pause.*) Have you got a
brick?

YOSSER. Not on me, no.

> *He shows the wino the photograph.*

If you see these on your travels, will you tell me?

WINO. They won't be where I'm going, pal. I'm going
somewhere dry. I'm gonna travel.

> *He gets up and moves to a shop window.*

YOSSER. They won't be in there.

WINO. If you break a window you get a cell for the night. You
get the evening as well. It's warm in a cell. and there's nae
mair rain.

> *He starts to sing and dance and kick at the window. He is joined by*
> *Yosser who has fetched a barrel from outside the pub next door.*
> *Yosser hurls the barrel straight through the window.*

WINO. That was my window.

> *They hear the alarm go off and are helpless to do anything except*
> *wait.*

41. Exterior. Williamson Square. Day.

There is now a police car in the Square. Its blue light revolving. The
police driver is smoking a cigarette. We hear, then see, the other
policeman in front of the broken window and between Yosser and the
wino. They are all talking at once.

WINO. It was me.

YOSSER. No it wasn't, it was me.

WINO. It wasn't, it was me. I did it. You caught me before I
could get away.

YOSSER. It was me.

POLICEMAN. (*To Yosser.*) Look, do me a favour – piss off. I know it's him, he's always at it. (*Turns to the wino.*) Come ahead, Jock . . .

Yosser takes hold of the policeman.

YOSSER. But it wasn't, it was me.

The policeman shoves him away. The policeman takes hold of the wino and pushes him towards the car.

YOSSER. But . . .

Yosser beings to follow them.

YOSSER. But . . .

He takes hold of the policeman's free arm but the policeman jerks away.

YOSSER. But . . .

They reach the police car. The policeman turns as Yosser takes hold of him again.

YOSSER. But . . .

POLICEMAN. Hey – don't 'but' me, alright?

We see a mad smile on Yosser's face. We leave the scene as he moves his head back.

42.   Exterior/Interior of police car. On the road. Day.

The policeman who has just been butted is holding a handkerchief to his nose. The handkerchief is blood-stained and he had a heavy nosebleed. His colleague is driving. The wino is singing again.

POLICEMAN. Shut it.

The wino stops singing and the policeman turns to Yosser speaking through his handkerchief.

POLICEMAN. You're dead you are, I'm tellin' y', dead.

Yosser turns to the wino.

YOSSER. I'm dead . . . I said I'm dead.

WINO. (*Not looking.*) Good. I'm glad.

YOSSER. So am I. I'm dead . . . but you smell.

WINO. I know.

YOSSER. That's all right then. (*He leans forward towards the policeman.*) Why am I dead?

POLICEMAN. You'll find out when I get you back to the station, now just shut up.

He is called up on the mobile radio telephone.

VOICE. Alpha Tango 23.

POLICEMAN. Alpha Tango 23. Go ahead.

VOICE. Alpha Tango 23, report of demonstration and possible riot at Aigburn Drive, Sefton Park area. Please investigate.

POLICEMAN. Alpha Tango 23. We're on our way. *(Puts receiver down.)*

The police car approaches Sefton Park with its siren going. It slows and the siren stops. We hear the policeman's voice.

POLICEMAN. Riots? What riots? Four old women with four old dogs, three flashers, five million bloody joggers and two head-bangers in the back. Alpha Tango 23 over and out.

He slams the receiver down.

YOSSER. I thought I knew where I was going once. I did. But there's nowhere left to go. 'Cos it's all . . .

WINO. Gone.

Yosser turns on him.

YOSSER. This is my conversation.

He turns back, the wino mumbles.

WINO. . . . I hate Scousers.

YOSSER. All right, I know it's my fault. I know I'm to blame. I know that. I know that much. But what I want to know is – is this all there is? Down to this. For the rest of my life. Hey?

The policeman pushes Yosser and gets hold of him by the back of the

Hey? Hey? Hey?

The policeman half turns and pushes Yosser backwards knocking him on to the seat. Yosser makes no attempt to retaliate, but sits back in the seat. He talks to himself and the others let him.

YOSSER. Not me. No chance. There's nothing down for me – and I'm not staying around for that. The trouble is most of us either talk to ourselves or through our arse. I've found that out. I'm thirty-six years old and I've found that out . . . Unless you're somebody. Somebody. And I bet it's crap for them an' all. I bet Graeme Souness is really unhappy.

There is a pause. Yosser scowls.

I bet.

The policeman who was butted is still blowing his nose tenderly. Yosser sees something out of the window. As the car approaches the lake in Sefton Park, Yosser looks at the policemen, half smiles then stops.

YOSSER. I'm going to be sick.

POLICEMAN. Oh shite . . .

YOSSER. Very . . . sick.

POLICEMAN. Not in here y' not.

He gestures to the driver and the police car slams to a halt. The policeman proceeds to drag Yosser out of the back of the car with Yosser talking all the while as he is bundled out and led to the side of the road.

YOSSER. Everything I've ever wanted, and all the things that I thought I had, they've all been taken away. I've got to take something. It's my turn.

The policeman pushes Yosser and gets hold of him by the back of the neck.

POLICEMAN. Just get on with it, will y'.

*He tries to push Yosser into a 'sick' position. Yosser straightens up
and shakes his head.*

YOSSER. I'm Yosser Hughes. And I can't stand it anymore.

*Yosser charges off towards the lake. The policeman follows him. The
driver gets out, stops and shouts into the car.*

POLICE DRIVER. You stay there.

As the driver joins the chase, the wino answers.

WINO. Where else would I be going?

*They both chase after Yosser who is hurtling towards the lake. The
policeman is close behind him, but stops as Yosser goes crashing
straight into the water and then on and on into the lake. The police
driver finally catches up. They both stand on the edge of the water,
bewildered. We see Yosser swimming wildly towards the centre of the
lake. He stops and treads water. Then he hurls himself under the
water. He emerges. We see the two policemen on the edge.*

POLICE DRIVER. He's . . .

POLICEMAN. Let the bastard die.

*We go back to Yosser who hurls himself under the water for a second
time, and for longer. He emerges spewing water.*

YOSSER. (*Howling.*) Come on, come on . . .

*When he goes down again, we hold for a long time and still there is
no sign. We go back to the policemen. They look at each other.*

POLICE DRIVER. Nah . . .

*The driver starts taking his jacket off, the other one hesitates and then starts
hurtling his jacket off in a tantrum. Yosser comes up and is visibly
upset about the fact. He hurls himself down again, and this time stays
down. From a distance we see the driver, followed by the other
policeman, reaching the spot where Yosser was. The driver dives down,
comes up and dives again. The other policeman paddles about. The
driver comes back up, holding Yosser by his jacket, half loses him,
then gets him again. Between them they start bringing Yosser towards*

shore, Yosser like a dead weight. Yosser is being hauled out of the lake. The two policemen go down on their knees. Yosser who is lying on his stomach appears unconscious or dead. The policemen get off their knees and pummel him desperately to resuscitate him. They go about their task with dedication, and in Nosebleed's case, physical violence. Eventually, Yosser opens his eyes. And finally he lifts his head and begins howling.

YOSSER. No no no. NO!

The final 'NO' is howled and reverberated. We freeze frame on his face, then zoom in tight on to his eye. Freeze. Silence then music.

George's Last Ride

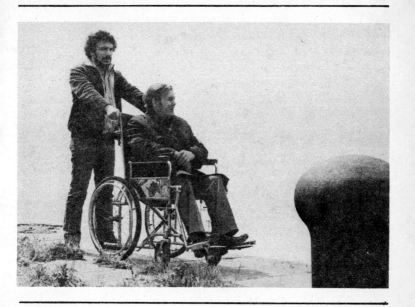

GEORGE MALONE   Peter Kerrigan
CHRISSIE TODD   Michael Angelis
YOSSER HUGHES   Bernard Hill
LOGGO LOGMOND   Alan Igbon
DIXIE DEAN   Tom Georgeson
KEVIN DEAN   Gary Bleasdale
MRS MALONE   Jean Heywood
RITCHIE MALONE   Tony Scoggo
JOHN MALONE   John Carrr
GRANDCHILDREN
Andrea Pruden
Tara Jones
Ian Jones
HOSPITAL DOCTOR   Ricky Tomlinson

FAMILY DOCTOR   Gwyll Williams
PRIEST   Mike Hayden
DOE CLERK   Isa Dixon
PUB MANAGER   Sam Kelly
SHAKE HANDS   Iggy Navarro
GLASS COLLECTOR   Eric Granville
'RONNY RENALDO'   Hans Lindhuber
GNASHER LLEWELLYN   A. T. Kossey
REDUNDANCY PARTY
Roger Phillips
Lorne Walker
Alan Junior
Al Conway
Steve Caldrow
Chris Benson
Billy Simons
YOUTHS IN PUB
Jo Braith
Peter Wilde
Tom Woods
Jeffrey Hoosen

1. Exterior. Department of Employment. Day.

We see the exterior of the DOE.

1a. Interior. Department of Employment. Main Hall. Day.

We see George's legs at the counter of the DOE. Then the female clerk's face. She is concerned, but barely able to look out front for more than a second. George is in cheerful mood.

GEORGE. Are you trying to tell me something, lass?

CLERK. . . . Mr Malone, you're wearing pyjamas. Again.

We see George. He doesn't look as though he is wearing pyjamas. He looks down at his jacket and feels it. Then he looks at the clerk.

CLERK. Pyjama bottoms.

GEORGE. That's my jogging gear.

CLERK. You'll catch your – you'll catch a cold like this. You know you will. Please Mr Malone, you know you shouldn't be here. Let me –

GEORGE. It's the tablets girl. They do your head in. I'm not gonna take them anymore.

She goes to the phone. He follows her to the grille.

Ah no, don't call an ambulance, girl.

He begins to back away.

I'm going home, they're not going to stop me. But if it makes you happy, I'll go back to the hospital first.

George walks away and goes through the doors. The clerk moves back to her position, then stands up and goes out after him.

2. Exterior, Department of Employment Building. Day

Dixie and Kevin approach along the pavement. They go up the steps and meet the counter-clerk who is coming out.

CLERK. Excuse me, you haven't seen an old feller in pyjamas, have you?

DIXIE. Yeah I saw him. He went down there, what's more he was riding a camel and carrying a handbag. You saw him didn't you Kev.

KEVIN. Yeah I saw him.

CLERK. Seriously.

DIXIE. *(Over his shoulder)* Are you going off your rocker behind that counter?

CLERK. George Malone.

DIXIE. George? But he's in hospital isn't he?

CLERK. He was, but he's just walked out of here wearing pyjamas.

DIXIE. You're joking?

CLERK. I'm not.

The clerk, Dixie and Kevin walk down the steps to look for George.

DIXIE. You're sure it's George?

CLERK. *Yes*, George Malone.

DIXIE. Which way did he go?

CLERK. I don't know.

And they walk along the pavement

DIXIE. *(To a passer-by)* You haven't seen George Malone have you?

3. Exterior. Albert Docks. Day.

We see George's feet and pyjama-clad legs. He coughs, and we see George's face, and then George's hand guiding himself down the steps, and along the edge of the dock.

Ritchie's wagon approaches. Ritchie is driving and John is sitting
next to him, with Chrissie and Loggo in the back of the wagon riding
'shotgun'. The van comes to a stop. We see George approach
an old capstan. We hear Loggo and Chrissie talking over this
action.

LOGGO. How did you know he'd be here?

    Chrissie laughs.

CHRISSIE. He spends more time here now than when he used
to work here.

    George turns an old wheel and then looks up to see the van. Ritchie
    and John are walking towards him.

RITCHIE. Dad . . . dad . . . dad. Y'not supposed to be here.

4. Exterior. Hospital. Day

Ritchie's wagon passes the Walton Hospital sign and turns into the hospital
grounds. When the van stops, John gets out. Then George struggles out of the
van and is helped towards the entrance by Ritchie and John.

5. Interior. Hospital Ward. Day.

The nurse walks into the wards towards George Malone who is in a hospital
bed, propped up on a pillow and now wearing a complete and matching set of
pyjamas, top and bottom. He is trying to look well, confident and cheerful.
But we can see that the bed next to his, nearest the ward door, is empty. A doctor
who is in his mid-thirties and who has a closed file in his hands is with him. He
also speaks with a suprisingly strong Liverpool 'rough and ready' accent.

DOCTOR. Anyway, you should be taking advantage of the rest
Mr Malone.

GEORGE. *(Coughs)* I don't like hospitals, doctor. It's as simple as
that. It's a tradition in our family, when y' went in hospital you
were as good as dead.

DOCTOR. Oh rubbish.

GEORGE. Especially when they put you in a bed near the corridor.

DOCTOR. It's an understandable fear, Mr Malone, but those days are long gone.

GEORGE. Try tellin' that to the feller who was in the next bed. You'd need a loudhailer though.

Another patient laughs. The Doctor looks at the laughing man then goes back to George.

DOCTOR. Mr James was extremely ill, and besides you really shouldn't be so pessimistic.

GEORGE. I'm not being pessimistic, I just want to go home. I felt great today and I've got a bit of work to do.

DOCTOR. Absolutely impossible.

GEORGE. Alright, I want to go out for a walk then.

DOCTOR. Mr Malone, you went for a walk yesterday, and—

GEORGE. Twice.

DOCTOR. Yes, twice, and the second time an ambulance had to bring you back.

GEORGE. They didn't give me a chance to get my second wind.

DOCTOR. I must insist.

GEORGE. And hiding my clothes is not going to make any difference, either, Sister.

DOCTOR. Oh . . . Mr Malone, you are not a healthy man. At the moment.

GEORGE. There you are then. Let me go home before I die.

DOCTOR. You're not going to die.

GEORGE. Oh? Immortality as well. That's a good offer, doctor.

Considering I'm on the National Health.

George grins at the doctor.

DOCTOR. Alright, listen to me. You've had surgery, right? From which it takes time to recover. You may need further surgery, I don't know. No one will know until we hear the results of the tests. And you can't expect to go back to work straightaway. The only thing your body wants at the moment is complete rest and recuperation. Surely you can understand that?

GEORGE. And I'm not taking any more of those head-banging tablets, Sister.

DOCTOR. I don't believe this, you really are an old sod, aren't you?

GEORGE. Yes.

George leans forward. He points.

'Do not go gentle into that good night, old age should
burn and rave at close of day.'

DOCTOR. 'Rage, rage against the dying of the light.'

GEORGE/DOCTOR. Dylan Thomas.

DOCTOR. 'Though wise men at their end know dark is right, because their words had forked – no lightning, they . . .'

GEORGE. Alright, smart arse.

DOCTOR. 'Do not go gentle.'

The Doctor stands, ruffles George's hair, laughs 'good night' then turns away. George talks as they move.

GEORGE. And what's more the food's a disgrace.

The Doctor laughs harder. The Sister follows him out.

6. Interior. Sister's office. Day.

*The Doctor and the Sister come into her room. There is a pause. The
Doctor sits by the window, then speaks tonelessly.*

DOCTOR. I lied to him, Sister. The results came through this
morning.

 The Sister looks at him.

Goodnight and Gold Bless. *(He pauses again.)* Oh shit and derision.
Sometimes I wish I was a vet.

Oh shit and derision. Sometimes I wish I was a vet.

 He walks out, as he finishes talking.

DOCTOR. I'm terribly sorry to tell you this, Mrs Malone, but
your dormouse is dying . . .

The Doctor and Sister leave the room.

7. Interior. Hospital Consulting Room. Day.

*The Doctor sits facing Mrs Malone in a small consulting room in the
hospital. Like George, she is in her early sixties. But she is well, well-
preserved, and well-dressed, without a trace of blue rinse or country life.*

DOCTOR. I would therefore suggest, in fact I would strongly
recommend, that more radical surgery should at least be
considered.

MRS MALONE. He doesn't want that. Doctor.

DOCTOR. It's not always a complete waste of . . . time. It can
very often give time.

MRS MALONE. He wants to go home.

DOCTOR. Yes I understand that. *(Pause)* Are you going to tell
him.

MRS MALONE. *(Quietly)* Surely it's obvious.

DOCTOR. . . . Pardon?

MRS MALONE. He already knows. That's why he wants to go home.

DOCTOR. *(Pause)* He keeps going on about his 'work', Mrs. Malone. But obviously he can never return to work.

MRS MALONE. He hasn't worked in eighteen months.

DOCTOR. Oh good. That's fine.

When she looks at him, the Doctor hesitates again.

No—er—I'm sorry. I mean it's . . . this is perhaps somewhat silly.

He laughs nervously.

But I—er—my father worked on the docks, Mrs Malone, and he was somewhat of a militant but there was a man there, he was the chairman of the shop stewards' committee. I went to a meeting he chaired once - my father took me, rather he made me go - I was only a boy at the time, eleven or twelve. It's twenty-five or maybe thirty years ago you understand.

He stumbles to a halt.

MRS MALONE. Yes, go on.

DOCTOR. Well this man's name was George Malone and the people in the hall kept chanting for him to speak, kept on and on till he did . . . I'm sorry. I just wondered if it was possibly the same person.

MRS MALONE. Oh aye, it's the same person. He was blacklisted in '58 and went to work on the blackstuff.

DOCTOR. The blackstuff?

MRS MALONE. The tarmac.

DOCTOR. Ah. The tarmac. Yes, well. I listened to him speak that night . . . like I'd never heard anyone speak before . . . or since. Of . . . one for all, and all for one. With the most tremendous passion . . .

MRS MALONE. Aye that's him.

DOCTOR. I've never forgotten it . . . My father spoke about him a lot. He said he was a great man.

MRS MALONE. He still is, doctor.

DOCTOR. Yes he still is.

He turns away from her.

Would you like to come through?

She nods, they rise and move towards the door. Mrs Malone speaks as they get outside the door.

MRS MALONE. Do you have any political beliefs doctor?

DOCTOR. Well yes, actually, I'm—er—very involved with the local Liberal Party. And the SDP, of course. *(He laughs.)* The Alliance, you know.

MRS MALONE. *(Lightly.)* Listening to my husband didn't really have that much effect then, after all?

She walks away.

We see the Doctor's reaction.

8. Interior. Hospital Ward. Day.

A nurse is looking out of the open window. She shouts 'Mr Malone'. Then she goes to George's empty bed where Mrs Malone joins her.

MRS. MALONE. Oh god!

DOCTOR. Oh, no, he seems to have disappeared. Again.

We see a flicker of a smile from Mrs Malone.

MRS MALONE I know where he'll be. It should have been our youngest son's birthday today.

9. Exterior. Cemetery. Day.

We see the words on Snowy's gravestone. George, in pyjama bottoms, slippers and donkey jacket, arrives at the headstone. He takes his cap off. Apart from George's hard breathing, as if he has just arrived after a long and tiring walk, there is silence. Then he laughs.

GEORGE. Ah son . . . son. It should be you stood here, talking to me . . . like a daft get.

> *Another pause. Silence.*

Oh son. Son son son. I never thought this would happen . . . but here I am, and I'd come every day. If I could. When you love your kids, you love them more than anything else in the whole wide friggin' world, and that's a fact.

> *Pause. He talks with anger.*

Oh Michael, I miss you son, I'd have willingly taken your place . . . I loved you . . . but if there's anything I can be glad about, we can be glad about, it's that we both knew it, son . . .

> *There is a long pause.*

Anyway Michael . . . Anyway. *(He tries to laugh.)* Oh Christ . . . I feel like James Stewart in 'Shenandoah'.

> *He stays still, his head resting on the headstone. We move back and away from him as he faces out. And we see an ambulance pulling up outside the graveyard.*

10. Exterior. George's House. Day.

The ambulance drives along the road and stops outside the house. We see the windows of several houses and people watching from doorways. Mrs Malone comes out on the pavement to welcome George who is returning home.

MRS MALONE. Hello love, hello pet. Welcome home.

> *One of the ambulancemen accompanying George has a small suitcase, the other offers to help him down from the back of the ambulance, but*

George protests and rejects the offer and that of a wheelchair. He walks out of the back of the ambulance. The ambulanceman takes the folded up wheelchair and they approach the house. Mrs Malone takes him inside, helped by the ambulancemen.

11. Interior. George's Living Room. Day.

Mrs Malone hangs up George's coat in the hall and enters the living room. The furniture is old-fashioned, traditional, with a definite sense of of *style and taste. There is also a coal fire blazing away. A huge bookcase stacked with books dominates the room. Even more books are stacked up on the floor, at both sides of and in front of the bookcase. George is seated on a chair with a footstool in front of it. He has several letters in his hand. Some official-looking ones, others obviously 'get well' cards. He opens the official ones first, as he talks. Mrs Malone goes to the table by the window to arrange the flowers, nodding as she listens.*

GEORGE. This is the stuff to give the troops. By god how I looked forward to this.

She looks at him quizzically and fetches a vase from the fireplace. He looks up.

Sitting here by my own fireside. With a clear head, and you.

He winks at her.

MRS MALONE. While you fight the good fight.

She crosses back to the table.

GEORGE. Well, among other things. But it keeps me occupied.

He looks up from the letter.

Hm, solicitor's letter. The landlord's solicitor.

MRS MALONE. Old Mr Farrell's house?

GEORGE. Listen to this. Execution of termination of tenancy. Eviction order. That's great isn't it. *(With irony, lightly.)* Congratulations on reaching the ripe old age of seventy nine, be out of the house within the month.

He looks down at the letter.

They want to know who I am, and what business is it of mine. They'll soon find out. *(He drops the letter down.)* Bastard landlords . . . and solicitors.

MRS MALONE. You can't do too much, George. Hardly anything. For a while.

GEORGE. Look, I can have a go. I'm not going to sit here and do crossword puzzles and stare at the four walls. *(He opens another letter.)* Ask Frank Farrell to come round will you please love, in the mornin' sometime.

MRS MALONE. *(Controlling herself, just.)* Look, George, I'm not going to stop you doing all this, but –

GEORGE. Have you ever?

MRS MALONE. But I am going to tell you when you've had enough.

GEORGE. I'll know that myself love.

He glances down at the letter.

MRS. MALONE. But that's the trouble – you won't.

George coughs. Pause.

You won't be able to help anyone if you get to the point where you can't help yourself.

GEORGE. Take it easy.

MRS MALONE. Oh aye.

He looks at the letter.

GEORGE. Young Katie, eh?

MRS MALONE. Chrissie's sister.

GEORGE. Yeah, she's got an appeals tribunal Wednesday week,

she'll want representing. I wonder if I . . .

He is already looking at his diary.

MRS MALONE. Be told will you, you can't go.

He holds his hands up in defeat.

GEORGE. Ok, Ok.

She looks disdainful and walks to the door.

MRS MALONE. John and Ritchie are coming over later.

GEORGE. Are the kids coming?

MRS MALONE. Yeah.

GEORGE. Great, while you're there love, fetch me that good pen of mine and that pad with the lines on.

She stares at him as he goes back to studying the letter.

GEORGE. Aye.

She goes out.

12. George's Living Room. Day.

We see George's remaining two sons, Ritchie and John, who are in their mid and late thirties, informally dressed, sitting at the table with George and his wife. They are just finishing a meal. But George has had soup only, and has taken his time with it. On the couch, the three grand-children are busy demolishing bowls of strawberry jelly. George stuggles at times for a breath and energy as he talks. Richie quietens the kids.

GEORGE. But that's what I'm telling you, that's why you've got to take them out, Ritchie. I mean, you know me, I was never one for taking men out if there was an option, especially if you had to take them back disillusioned and empty-handed.

RITCHIE. You know the score, dad.

GEORGE. But men can't work under those conditions.

RITCHIE. I know, dad. But look, times are hard now, let's face it. And most of them don't want to come out because they're thinking of their few bob.

GEORGE. Money before safety.

JOHN. That's the way it is.

JOHN. It's different now, dad. These days, y'go out on strike —

RITCHIE. Whatever the reasons –

JOHN. . . . before y'can get out of the gates, management are havin' sing songs an' wearing party hats.

RITCHIE. *(Indicating.)* With 'Goodbye Boys' written on the front.

JOHN. Come back next week to get your cards.

GEORGE. But what are the men thinking about? Y' not goin' to tell me that they're safeguardin' their future – 'cos they've got none whatever way it goes – so they may as well do what's right an' honest.

He coughs, Anna looks up.

RITCHIE. *(Holding his hands up.)* Look dad, I stood there yesterday, right John . . .

JOHN. Yeah.

RITCHIE. . . . .said to them I said, look – this workshop is a deathtrap, one of youse is going to get killed and it won't be a finger or a thumb next time, it'll be a two hundredweight of bloody mince meat lyin' there. They just looked at me.

JOHN. They just stood there, lookin' around, wonderin' who they'd like it to be.

RITCHIE. On the floor.

JOHN. As long as it wasn't them.

RITCHIE. I tell y', dad , honest to god – I look around sometimes at some of the fellers I'm supposed to be fightin' for . . . they don't seem to care or understand about anythin' that hasn't got tits or comes from a barrel. I mean that.

GEORGE. No, no, no. You're wrong!

RITCHIE. I mean it.

MRS MALONE. *(Flaring – starts clearing the table.)* And I won't have that kind of defeatist talk at my table. Go and eat jelly with the bairns go on. And on your way to work in the morning, buy the *Daily Mail.*

JOHN. Ah come on mam, we were just –

MRS MALONE. Talking soft – that's what you were doing, have had it soft most of your lives.

   The brothers exchange glances.

Talk to me about hardship and want. Talk to me about no shoes on your feet. Have you any idea what no shoes on your feet means?

JOHN. It means getting y' feet wet when it rains.

RITCHIE. And your socks go mouldy.

JOHN. It means the thirties mam, and soup kitchens and hunger marches. You with your father marchin' from the North East, and my dad with his. It means people standing together and fighting. And it means another time and age.

MRS MALONE. And the only reason things got better was because of men like your father, who refused to be slave labour and cannon fodder, who said 'No, I won't go down the docks every morning and stand in a stinking pen, and no I won't beg for half a day's work and come crawling home defeated.'

   She leaves the table and goes into the kitchen. She continues her speech
   when she comes back in.

And what's it got better for? so the likes of you can sit back and say you can't do nothing and let it all happen to us again.

   She storms out of the room, having cleared the contents of the table,
   except for George's soup bowl.

JOHN. What did you let her read Karl Marx for, dad?

GEORGE. Dickens.

RITCHIE. Pardon?

GEORGE. Tale of Two Cities. We are the most important part of the nation. We are the ones who do the work.

He coughs heavily. Pause. John's daughter, Anna, a girl of seven, approaches. She looks at George carefully.

GEORGE. What can I do for you Anna babe?

ANNA. Are you really going to die, grandad?

A brief gob-smacked silence. They all look at each other fast, then away.

GEORGE. It has been known to happen.

ANNA. What's it like?

JOHN. Enough, enough. Sssshh, sshssshhssshh.

GEORGE. Nobody knows, kidder. It's like . . . .the next episode of . . . Spiderman. Nobody knows what it's like . . . until it happens.

ANNA. I don't like Spiderman.

GEORGE. Neither do I.

He hugs her, she goes.

RITCHIE. Come on kids. Who wants more jelly?

They cheer. We hear John's voice.

JOHN. Come on, Anna. Back to the jelly love.

They all go into the kitchen. George stares out. Mrs Malone walks back in. He pushes the bowl of soup away. He hasn't touched it. She takes the bowl.

GEORGE. Lovely soup that . . .

George looks at her then away, Mrs Malone shakes her head and walks to the kitchen.

13. Interior. George's Bedroom. Night.

The room is functional, old-fashioned, with nothing new, plastic or expensive. The light from a lamp post struggles through the window and the curtains. In their big double bed, Mrs Malone is lying awake, staring out. George is asleep, his breathing difficult but regular. Suddenly his body jerks slightly, he groans, and appears to stop breathing for a fraction. Mrs Malone throws herself across him. And wakes him up.

MRS MALONE. George!

GEORGE. What?

He turns over and goes to sleep again.

MRS MALONE. Nothing. It's . . . alright.

She scratches her hands nervously and studies the ceiling.

14. Interior. George's Living Room. Day.

We see the coal fire. We see Yosser sitting down and facing out. He is dressed in clean clothes, is washed and shaved with his hair brushed back, almost too manically, away from his face. He is wearing a grey scarf around his neck.

YOSSER. Me mother took me in. In the end . . . me mother.

Silence. We see George again. There is a cup and saucer at his side. He looks far from well. He takes his glasses off.

GEORGE. I'm sorry, Yosser, I know you've got your problems, but come to the point son.

YOSSER. I'm better now, George. I reached bottom but . . . I'm better now. Better than I was. I'm getting better all the time . . . *(He leans forward confidently.)* I can see things.

GEORGE. What can you see?

YOSSER. . . . How do you mean? *(Pause.)* I want my children back. That's what I want.

GEORGE. Go to the social services and talk quietly, behave properly, get the case re-opened, custody of the kids, explain your position. Your ma's a good woman. Show them where you live and how you're living.

Yosser looks away.

YOSSER. I haven't got a chance then.

GEORGE. Look Yosser, I know you . . . love your kids but you can't inflict your bitterness and hurt on them. Or anyone else, for that matter. Once you've broken something you can't break it again. You've just got to start picking up the pieces.

Yosser nods.

YOSSER. Why do you know everything?

George laughs but it turns to coughing. Yosser gets up, crosses to where George is sitting and picks him up.

GEORGE. Put me down, you big soft sod! *(Yosser puts him down.)* I don't know everything. I hardly know bugger all. I just try and apply the little bit I know, and what I learn. To some useful purpose. That's all.

YOSSER. I want to be like that. I want to be someone . . . just that. *(He looks down.)*

GEORGE. Be yourself, Yosser, that's all, just be yourself.

Yosser looks up. George is obviously in pain. Yosser crosses to the door.

YOSSER: But what happens if you don't like yourself? . . .

Yosser goes out.

15. Interior. George's Back Living Room. Day.

Yosser comes to the doorway and opens the door to reveal George's waiting room, in the back living room of the house. Seated are the old man, Frank Farrell, a middle-aged lady, a man in his thirties, and a young woman, drinking tea silently like any waiting room with a tea machine.

YOSSER. Next. *(He laughs.)* Next please!

*Suddenly there is a sound of the cup and saucer smashing in the living
room, followed by a quiet thud. Yosser turns and goes back into the
hallway towards the front living room. Yosser calls 'Mary! Mary!'
Frank Farrell follows her. We see Mrs Malone in the kitchen at the
sink, washing potatoes. She turns.*

16. Interior. George's Bedroom. Day.

*George is in bed, asleep. Mrs Malone, both her sons and a doctor are
standing by the bed. The doctor closes his bag.*

DOCTOR. *(His tone is soft.)* I'll pop back before evening surgery.
See how he is. Alright?

The doctor goes out with John. Silence.

RITCHIE. That's it, mam, y'know. He can't see anyone else. *(We
see George asleep.)* No one else's bastard problems. He's got
enough of his own. And I'll stand by that front door and stop
them if need be.

*She silently agrees. Ritchie crosses over to Mrs Malone puts his hands
on her shoulders.*

Oh mam.

*Ritchie glances out of the window. Chrissie and Loggo are just
arriving as the doctor is leaving.*

It's Chrissie and Loggo.

*He goes. Chrissie talks to the doctor outside. We stay in the room
with Mrs Malone and George. She goes and sits on the bed. As
George wakes up and looks up at his wife, she takes his hand.*

GEORGE. Oh Mary, Mary. What am I doing to you? I'm sorry,
girl. I'm in terrible pain, girl. . . . it's me stomach, it's
just . . . it's gone. And the worst thing . . . I'm so helpless.

Mrs Malone looks at him.

I can't, I've got . . . no energy. What am I doing to you?

She wipes his face with her hand and looks away.

17. Exterior. George's House. Saturday. Midday.

We see Chrissie closing the front door. George is in the wheelchair outside the door.

CHRISSIE. I'll see you, Mary.

Chrissie starts pushing George towards the side of the road and the dead docks of the south side. George is unable to raise his voice, and when he does become enthusiastic he pays heavily for it.

CHRISSIE. Alright ace.

GEORGE. What a great day Chrissie.

CHRISSIE. Where are we going.

GEORGE. What about the Baltic? Can you get there do you think?

CHRISSIE. Yeah, well, we're going there anyway.

They go down the street seen through the railings. The docks are deserted.

GEORGE. I wouldn't have believed it, you know, Chrissie. Look at it.

CHRISSIE. . . . Look at what?

GEORGE. Saturday dinnertime. Not a soul about. Once upon a time, Chrissie . . . once upon a time . . .

CHRISSIE. If you're going to tell me about Cinderella, I'm taking you home now.

We see them walk along the pavement above the dead docks. Each phase of George's speech is shot in a different area of wasteland and indiscriminate destruction until we reach their destination.

18. Exterior. Dock Area. Day.

George is being pushed by Chrissie along the bridge leading to the dead docks.

GEORGE. Saturday afternoon. We'd have been looking forward

to it from the previous Saturday – payday Saturday you know –
no five-day week and off to the Leisure Centre then, boyo. Ah,
there'd be hundreds of us coming along here, the ship repair
men, scalers, dockers, the Mary Ellens who used to swab the big
liners, and behind us the great big Shire cart horses.

They walk through a huge scrapyard full of rusty metal.

Ah Chrissie, and there were many a good old horse
who walked down the hill with us who came back up in the
knackers' carts. The vet'd put a gun to his head and a straw
bolster around its neck, and wind it up into the knacker's cart,
and its big head turning. You could still see the whites of its
eye . . . and yet the horses of privilege that pose outside
Buckingham Palace and ponce and parade up and down the
Mall were turned out into a meadow of cowslip and clover and
guaranteed a full proven bag for the rest of their lives.

They reach the waterfront along the River Mersey.

Ah Chrissie it just seems like soddin' yesterday, the midday gun. The
women sandstoning the steps and the flags. The kids playing alley oh,
the little shops on the corner where you got the three pennyworth of
fine irish, the old snuff, and the twist of tobacco, and your old
gran had a flat top cart there, used to sell salt fish and a big
barrel of ribs, straight off the pig's back from the Irish boats
and on the third Saturday an organ grinder and his
monkey . . .

19. Exterior. Docks.

They continue along the waterfront.

GEORGE. And there we'd be pilin' into Effin' Nellie's or Peg-leg
Pete's, for a couple of pints of good beer, maybe the first in the
week and the crack . . . the crack . . . we'd talk of many
things . . .

We hear Chrissie's voice.

CHRISSIE. Of cabbages and Kings.

They walk through a derelict warehouse in the Albert Docks and look up at the rafters.

GEORGE. Of politics and power and come the day when we'd have inside toilets and proper bathrooms. Of Attlee and Bevan, Hogan and Logan, the Braddocks and Dixie Dean . . . and Lawton and Liddell and Matthews and Finney . . . of Come the Revolution and the Blackpool Illuminations . . . Joseph Jones had a violin, a 'Stradavarious', he said . . .

20. Exterior. Container Base. Day.

We see George and Chrissie going silently through a container base on the Dock Road, past row upon row of containers, being dwarfed by them. A stacker-truck passes them by. A flock of birds takes off in front of them.

21. Exterior. The Albert Docks. Day.

George and Chrissie are now in the same setting as in the third scene, surrounded by beautiful, derelict ruins. George is sitting in the wheelchair, Chrissie is pushing him.

GEORGE. Well we've got our bathrooms . . . At considerable expense . . . I write letters to prison for the mother of a man who rapes little boys, but there's hundreds of friggin' rapists still running free.

George waves to Chrissie to stop. They do.

GEORGE. Get me up, son. Get me up, Chrissie.

CHRISSIE. Are you sure, George?

GEORGE. Yeah.

Chrissie comes around to the front of the wheelchair. He lifts George up, gently, then holds him in his arms and hugs him. Long and hard. When he releases George, George just looks at him and nods once. He doesn't need to ask. Chrissie stands him up against the wall and holds him there.

GEORGE. Forty-seven years ago. I stood here, a young bull, and watched my first ship come in . . . They say that memories live longer than dreams . . . But my dreams, those dreams, those dreams of long ago, they still give me some kind of hope and faith in my class . . . I can't believe there is no hope, I can't.

He just stares out.

CHRISSIE. Hey, come on, George, your lads'll be in the Baltic Fleet now, you know. Pints on the bar . . . Loggo said he might come over . . .

We see Chrissie getting George back in the wheelchair.

CHRISSIE. Christ George, you're getting heavy.

Chrissie puts George's feet on the footrest. Chrissie is on his haunches looking at George.

CHRISSIE. George . . .

George is sitting completely still. Chrissie reaches to touch his face, almost to feel his breath, but doesn't.

CHRISSIE. They'll be waiting for us you know George.

Chrissie looks round over his shoulders.

CHRISSIE. Oh Jesus.

Chrissie then suddenly stands up, turns and runs. First one way, then the other. And runs. And runs. From a distance, we see George in the wheelchair and Chrissie running along the derelict dockside. Slow fade to black.

22. Interior. George's Bedroom. Night.

Pan up from black to see Mrs Malone with George's body in a coffin on a stand. The coffin, which hasn't yet been closed, is barely seen in the shadows. Mrs Malone is sitting still and erect on a hard-backed chair facing the bed.

23. Interior. George's Bedroom. Day.

Daylight comes in through the drawn curtains on to the candle, crucifix and madonna on the table. Then a knock at the bedroom door. The door opens. Ritchie comes in.

RITCHIE. . . . They're here, Mam.

She nods.

24.   Interior. George's Living Room. Day.

The room, which is wildly overcrowded, is full of people looking at the carpet. We see Mrs Malone go by the doorway with Ritchie. John comes into the room.

JOHN. . . . First car.

As the mourners troop out of the living room, we see Chrissie and Loggo in there at the back. They look through the curtains then walk out. We see sitting alone on a couch, hidden until now, George's grand-daughter, Anna. She is eating a packet of crisps as tears silently trip her. She keeps eating through the tears.

25. Exterior. George's House. Day.

The curtains are drawn in every house in the street. People line the street, some still coming out of the houses. We see the funeral cars, and a line of cars behind them. The procession of cars sets off down the road. Yosser is standing silently in the road, apart from the crowd. Head down, he starts walking with the procession. We see Ritchie, John and Mrs Malone in the first car as it follows the hearse. We see old men taking their caps off, women blessing themselves, people waving strange little waves, like children. As the car carrying George goes past them an old lady stumbles towards the car, crying 'God rest you son, God be with you,' and is lead away. Mrs Malone is upset and calmed by Ritchie and John.

MRS MALONE. Bless her.

RITCHIE AND JOHN. It's alright Mum.

26. Interior. The Church. Day.

*We see three altar boys walk down the aisle to the altar. The younger
two are chatting and are told to 'be quiet' by the older one. They place
the candles on the altar table and the crucifix against the wall. They
stand by the wall. John, Ritchie and Chrissie and three older men carry
the coffin down the aisle towards the altar, followed by the close
mourners. The congregation is standing, filling the pews. The priest is
walking ahead of the cofin.*

PRIEST. Show your mercy, Lord, to this departed servant of
yours. Since he strove to do your will, let him not be punished
for wrongdoing. And as he was united in the true faith with all
your faithful people, let him now by your loving goodness be
united with the angelic throng. Through Christ our Lord. I
know that my Redeemer lives, and that on the last day I shall
rise again; and in my flesh I shall see God, my Saviour. I
myself shall see Him: with my own eyes I shall gaze upon Him: And
in my flesh I shall see God, my Saviour. This is the hope which is laid up
in my heart: And in my flesh I shall see God, my Saviour.

> *The priest turns, as the coffin reaches the step to the altar. The
> funeral attendants take the coffin from the bearers and place it on the
> trestles. We see Dixie and Kevin and Loggo among the rows of
> familiar faces. At the back of the church we see Yosser enter, and
> stand against the wall. The close mourners file into the pews at the
> front of the church, and the family sit in the front pew. The
> congregation are standing. Mrs Malone and the children wait. The
> priest blows his nose. The coffin is lowered onto the trestles. Chrissie
> watches. The funeral attendants bow. The priest turns and approaches
> the altar, genuflects, kisses it and starts the service. The altar boys
> chat briefly then concentrate.*

PRIEST. In the name of the Father and of the Son and of the
Holy Spirit Amen. The Grace of our Lord Jesus Christ and
the love of God and the fellowship of the Holy Spirit be with
you all.

CONGREGATION. And also with you.

PRIEST. My brothers and sisters, to prepare ourselves to celebrate the sacred mysteries, let us call to mind our sins.

We cut outside to see the three funeral cars outside the church. The drivers are having a smoke, reading newspapers and cleaning the car windows. We come back into the church.

PRIEST. Rejoice and be glad for your reward will be great in Heaven, this is how they persecuted the prophets before you. This is the Gospel of the Lord.

CONGREGATION. Praise to you Lord Jesus Christ.

Congregation sit automatically.

PRIEST. *(To Yosser)* Please sit down.

Yosser just stands in the middle of the aisle. The priest withers him. Yosser moves back and sits on the end of a pew making someone move up for him. Loggo turns round and sees Yosser sit.

PRIEST. My dear friends, may I say that I have never seen so many people gathered here to pay their last respects. I am sure that the family of Patrick Malone must –

Ritchie stands and interrupts the priest. He is tight-lipped and angry.

RITCHIE. George Malone. My father's name was George.

PRIEST. I'm sorry. *(He quickly looks down at his notes just to make sure. Ritchie sits.)* But he was christened here in this very Church as Patrick, and that is his name as known to Almighty God.

Ritchie stands again.

RITCHIE. I don't care what his name was known by under Almighty God. Patrick Malone means nothing to the people here. His name was George Malone. That's how he was known by all of us. George Malone.

He sits and suddenly puts his head down. His mother quietly takes his hand, while still staring out.

PRIEST. . . . I am sure that the family of George Malone must

be proud of the recognition and respect accorded to this man.
To George Malone. The Acts of the Apostles perhaps best sum
up the affect that this one man's life must have had on all who
met him. It says in the Acts of the Apostles, 'Silver and gold
have I none; but such as I have, give I thee.' From what I
have learnt of Pa – George Malone, I believe that this noble
and fine sentiment pertains to him.

He switches to automatic pilot.

Of one thing be certain, however, and at this sad time,
when by nature of why we are gathered here this morning, we
must be aware of our own mortality, let us remember that we
are all children of Almighty God, we are all here on this good
earth till He calls us to Him, and we must always, in the word
of the Lord, 'stand ready, because the Son of Man is coming at
an hour you do not expect.' And with this in mind, I would
like to remind you of my earlier reading from the Romans,
Chapter 14 verses 7 to 12 . . .

*And as the Priest goes on to describe the joys of mortality, death and
judgement, we see Ritchie and John glaring at the priest, getting more
and more tense. The other people on the front pew exchange glances,
except for Mrs Malone, who bows her head. By the end of the speech,
Chrissie and John are having to hold Ritchie down.*

. . . The life and death of each of us has its influence
on others. If we live, we live for the Lord; and if we die, we
die for the Lord. This explains why Christ both died and came
to life, it was so that he might be Lord both of the dead and
the living. This is also why you should never pass judgement on
a brother or treat him with contempt. We shall have to stand
before the judgement seat of God; as scripture says: Be my life –
it is the Lord who speaks – every knee shall bend before me,
and every tongue shall praise God. It is to God, therefore, that
each of us must give an account of –

*Chrissie stand up and speaks. He hates every second, but he has to say
it. As he speaks we also see Angie, his wife, in the pew behind him.*

CHRISSIE. I'm sorry Father, but you're not on. We haven't come
here to listen to this. The last thing I want to do is to stand up

and interrupt you, but you'd better know – we're all here today not to send George to a better place or a judgement day, or to worry about our own going, but to remember his life and curse the fact that he's not here. He was a good man. He was the best man I ever knew. I . . . I loved George Malone, and our lives are going to be a lot emptier now that he's not here. he didn't do nothing for no rewards. Not here, nor in . . . Heaven.

> *Chrissie sits down, head down. Ritchie puts his hands on Chrissie's. We see the priest. He finally speaks with some semblance of dignity and awareness.*

PRIEST. Well . . . yes. It would appear that Church has very little to do here but to pay its own respects to George Malone. And I understand that. I am aware of the intensity. Of feeling. A good life lost has little compensation. To those who remain . . . In the name of the Father and of the Son and of the Holy Ghost.

27. Exterior. Cemetery. Day.

There is a large crowd of mourners. The coffin is in the ground. The priest has said the end of the burial service. The grave-digger gives the family some earth. They throw it into the grave, and go. Mrs Malone is left alone with her grief as people start to move away from the grave. Ritchie, John and Chrissie comfort each other. At this point we hear Mrs. Malone fall onto the coffin from the graveside. We see Chrissie, Ritchie and John fetch her out, helped by the hospital doctor. They walk with her and the other mourners to the cars. We see Yosser, a lone figure on higher ground. He turns and walks away.

28. Interior. George's Living Room. Day.

After the funeral. Ham and tuna and cheese sandwiches are being handed round by old ladies, as well as madeira cake, cups of tea, sherry and whisky. We see children eating, and groups of men clustered in the corners, with the women sitting around, or standing in similar groups. The priest is alone, drinking whisky quickly. John enters the room. He talks to no one in particular.

JOHN. No bones broken. She's alright.

There is a murmur of relief. John goes into the front room. Loggo and Chrissie stand together. Chrissie, Loggo, then John come into the back room. Someone is humming, the priest is in the background drinking. John looks over at the priest who says 'a decent man George' to Loggo and Chrissie. Chrissie glances at Loggo. He indicates out, Loggo nods, they go. The priest puts his glass down. Loggo and Chrissie go to the front door, but when they open it, they stop. They see Yosser, across the road on the other pavement. staring at George's house.

LOGGO. *(Turning away.)* Oh frig!

CHRISSIE. Out the back.

They close the door. We see Yosser closer.

29. Interior. George's Back Kitchen. Day.

They go into the back kitchen to reach the back door. We see John and Ritchie alone as a woman goes past carrying a tray of tea. Both brothers are sitting sombrely side by side at the back kitchen table. 'One of us will have to stay here with her, that's for sure.' They see Loggo and Chrissie and immediately stand up. Loggo ducks towards the back door.

LOGGO. Ok lads. See you again. Look after yourselfs.

RITCHIE. Thank you lads.

Chrissie puts his hands up.

CHRISSIE. No sweat. Take care of yourselves.

JOHN. Take it easy, lads.

Chrissie too ducks out as fast as he can before the brothers can approach and thank him.

30. **Exterior. Back yard. Day.**

*We see the priest on his knees. He has been sick into a grid. We see
Chrissie behind. Loggo, waiting for Chrissie, loosens his collar and watches
the priest. Chrissie also looks at the priest then moves off. Loggo
nods to Chrissie and goes into the alleyway. Chrissie follows. They walk
down the alleyway from the camera.*

CHRISSIE. Have we got much on this afternoon?

LOGGO. Not a lot.

CHRISSIE. How much money have we got?

LOGGO. Enough.

CHRISSIE. Good. 'Cos I'm going to get arseholed.

31. **Interior. Pub. Day.**

*We see the interior of the public bar, and it is not a pretty sight:
bedlam alive and well. It is just after midday of a Thursday. There is
a pool table and fruit machine on the go. 'Imagine' has been on the
jukebox and people are still singing it. A vociferous game of cards is in
progress in a barely seen corner. We see 'If I Were a Blackbird' being
whistled and sung by Ronny Renaldo. He is sitting near Gnasher
Llewellyn and his dummy. Every so often he sings and whistles 'If I
Were a Blackbird', we hardly focus on him or Gnasher until they
perform. The television is showing a wild life programme. But the sound
has been turned down. We focus briefly on an elderly waiter/glass
collector, who is doing his job slightly faster than he should be. He
repeats continually 'Empty your glasses, please' and when he has
collected all the glasses up, he puts them back on the tables and
starts again. As the scene develops, the speed at which he
operates increases, and at every chance he drinks the dregs from
the bottom of each glass, making a yodelling noise as he does
so. It is all a madness understated.*

LOGGO. That's what I like about this place, Chrissie – it's
nice and quiet at lunchtimes.

*Loggo and Chrissie are at the bar getting their drinks. They grin at
each other. Loggo indicates Dixie and Kevin, who now come into our
view. Chrissie and Loggo move down the bar towards them. We also
see the pub manager at the optic, taking pills. In a pop-eyed manner.*

LOGGO. Alright fellas!

CHRISSIE. Alright lads!

CHRISSIE. I thought you went away Kev.

KEVIN. I did.

CHRISSIE. What happened?

KEVIN. I came back.

Silence. Kevin and Dixie finish their drinks.

LOGGO. Do you fellas want another or what?

DIXIE. Not from you two, no.

Dixie starts to move away, followed by Kevin.

CHRISSIE. Ah come on, Dix . . .

But Dixie and Kevin walk out.

LOGGO. Well you can't win them all.

*The bar room door opens again. They both look across and then
rapidly away and down.*

LOGGO. Oh shite, not 'Shake-hands'!

*We see 'Shake-hands', a big man in his early forties, in trim. When
he speaks it is a hoarse whisper like a man with a serious throat
disorder or a fixation with Marlon Brando's performance in 'The
Godfather'. The manager pops his pills when he sees Shake-hands too.
Shake-hands approaches the bar and Loggo and Chrissie.*

SHAKE-HANDS. Shake hands.

LOGGO. *(Not looking.)* I've got dermatitis, Shakes.

SHAKE-HANDS. *(Same intonation.)* Shake hands.

*Loggo offers him his hand, wincing already. Shake-hands shakes
hands, with both his hands. Loggo groans with pain.*

SHAKE-HANDS. What d' you want?

LOGGO. An ambulance *(Shake-hands grins broadly.)* Pint of bitter,
Shakes.

*Shake-hands faces the bar, speaks to absolutely nobody, very quietly,
just in case someone is there and hiding.*

SHAKE-HANDS. Pint of bitter, boss.

COLLECTOR. *(Hurrying past.)* Empty y' glasses now please! *(We
see him in action.)* Come on, ladies, let's have your glasses please.

LOGGO. At ten past twelve!

*Loggo blows on his injured hand. Shake-hands is now out of view,
but we can still hear him.*

SHAKE-HANDS. Shake hands.

*The manager re-appears, quietly twitching, heavily harassed and totally
worn out.*

MANAGER. *(Half-hearted.)* Oh come on, Shakes. You're barred
out.

SHAKE-HANDS. Shake hands.

MANAGER. But I'll let you off this time. What y'havin'?

SHAKE-HANDS. *(Louder.)* Pint of bitter please, Joseph, thank you
very much.

*Only Shake-hands gets a drink. The collector comes back. We see the
four youths in the corner laughing.*

COLLECTOR. Let's have your glasses now, please!

*As he speaks, he snatches Loggo's unfinished pint of bitter. As Loggo
goes to pick it up we see the collector drinking it as he hurries away.*

LOGGO. What's up with him?

MANAGER. Those dick-heads over there slipped some speed into
the slops *(We see the youths again.)* knowin' full well he drinks
the dregs. I tried to lock him in the toilet before but he broke
the bloody door down.

SHAKE-HANDS. That's not nice. I like Harold. He's my friend.

Meanwhile, out of view, Ronny Renaldo has once again started whistling and singing 'If I Were a Blackbird I Would Whistle and Sing'. The glass collector is putting bottles on the youth's table when Shake-hands walks over, faces the four youths and challenges them.

SHAKE-HANDS. Shake hands.

But we stay with Loggo, Chrissie and the manager and hear Shake-hands saying, louder this time, 'Shake hands now!'

MANAGER. *(Sighs.)* Has he had a go at yours, as well?

CHRISSIE. Er—yeah.

Chrissie and Loggo exchange knowing glances. Although we can't see Shake-hands, we can still hear him: 'Shake hands, shake hands now.'
Then, still out of view, the first youth screams. The manager tops up Chrissie's pint.

MANAGER. I tell y'. I'll be glad when I'm gone. I've been due a move for nearly nine months but they can't get anyone else to come here.

The manager look over to the youths table as the second youth screams.

MANAGER. I wouldn't mind but –

He looks across towards Shake-hands.

SHAKE-HANDS. Pint of bitter for the boy.

The manager looks regularly and very quickly at the scene. And at the same time, at every opportunity, he slips a double whisky into the glass he's already got.

MANAGER. I wouldn't mind but –

Again, Shake-hands' voice carries from across the room. It is now very loud.

SHAKE-HANDS. Am I talking to myself? Shake hands.

MANAGER. And if I find out who's bringing the home brew in here . . .

YOUTH: *(Unseen.)* Aaaaah! Get off.

The manager is now drinking hard and fast.

MANAGER. I wouldn't mind, but three years ago –

He looks across as we hear screams of pain from the area round Shake-hands. He pours himself another whisky as he talks, hesitates and then turns it into a double.

MANAGER. Three years ago . . .

SHAKE-HANDS. *(Unseen.)* Make that two pints. Shake hands.

MANAGER. . . . three years ago, this was a quiet pub. There was only . . . there was only fights at the weekends and weddings.

Out of sight, the third youth gives a groan of pain.

MANAGER. I mean if they go . . .

The manager looks over to the lads, then double-takes. We see Shake-hands with the third youth who slumps to the floor.

SHAKE-HANDS. Make that three pints, boss.

MANAGER. . . . If they got legless they danced on the tables. Now they break them over each others' heads. Someone is bringing home-brew in here y'know. I know they are.

The glass-collector approaches.

COLLECTOR. Empty your glasses please.

Loggo and Chrissie close up to protect their glasses. The collector tries to grab them but it repulsed.

MANAGER. They've all got too much time to kill, that's what it is.

We see Shake-hands pursuing a fourth lad who hides under the table. table.

SHAKE-HANDS. Shake hands. Am I talking to myself?

FOURTH YOUTH. Get lost will you?

SHAKE-HANDS. Shake hands.

FOURTH YOUTH. Pick on someone your own size.

Shake-hands turns the table over and chases the youth to the window.
We hear him say 'Shake hands' as, yet again, Ronny Renaldo bursts
into song.

MANAGER. Let's face facts, boys, it's bedlam in here. Just look at them, just friggin' look at them.

Shake-hands pulls the fourth youth off the window ledge onto the
floor. There are shouts of 'Leave the kid alone!' As the youth cries
'Oh me bum!'

MANAGER. Just take a look around – we all had something to give. I mean Gnasher, over there, Gnasher *(Over Ronny's whistling.)* He never gnashed until Tate and Lyle laid him off. And Ronny over there was a waiter at the Adelphi. The last thing he did was rob the uniform when he left, had no time for his friggin' whistlin' – then.

The manager takes money for the next pint from Loggo, walks
towards the till, stops, and pockets the money. He turns back.

MANAGER. Shake-hands – he was a bouncer in town. At least two of those kids had apprenticeships. Everyone was either respectable or a villain.

COLLECTOR. *(Out of view.)* Hurry along there please. Haven't you got homes to go to? *(He makes a noise like a train.)*

The manager has another drink then continues his speech.

MANAGER. They had good reason to get pissed. Now they just get pissed 'cos they wish they were dead.

Another drink.

And so do I.

He looks across at the mayhem and helps himself to more whisky.

After all, this is only buildin' up for Saturday night.

Suddenly, the redundancy party arrives: six big redundant men enter
the pub.

FIRST MAN. *(Already half-cut.)* Set them up, Joe! This is going to be a night to end all nights!

The manager heads for the whisky.

MANAGER. Oh shite, not another redundancy party.

He crosses to the optic, then looks round.

FIRST MAN. Listen, Joey. Come here mate I want four bitters . . .

MANAGER. Every single one barred out already. What am I going to do?

The manager does the whisky into a treble. The men are at the bar. The first man is shouting his order still.

MANAGER. (*To himself.*) The manager of the Eagle's got a shotgun . . . (*Then he turns to Chrissie and Loggo.*) I'd only shoot myself if I had one. (*He turns to the redundancy party.*) What?

FIRST MAN. Listen Joey, come on listen, come on! I want four bitters, a golden and a lager, plus five whiskys and a gin an' tonic for the puff.

SECOND MAN. (*Six foot nine and seventeen stone.*) Leave off, bollocks . . .

FIRST MAN. (*Putting a roll of money on the counter.*) There y'are, Joey. When that's gone, let us know. What do you want fellas?

The manager takes the money.

CHRISSIE. (*Watching it all.*) Time to go, Loggo.

LOGGO. Hang on, Chrissie, let me finish my pint.

FIRST MAN. (*Turning to the room.*) What d'y'want fellers? Anything y'want!

LOGGO. No you're alright Mick we're sound.

FIRST MAN. Come 'head, Loggo, what's up with y' - y'look as though y've been to a funeral.

Loggo and Chrissie look at each other. Chrissie raises his eyebrows slightly.

FIRST MAN. Look, boys. I've got a grand here. Once it's gone, it's gone, frig it.

LOGGO. No y' alright, Mick, we're in.

FIRST MAN. Y'can be in again, can't y'. Two more pints over here, Joey.

He goes. Now Shake-hands is approaching the bar, flexing his fingers.

SHAKE-HANDS. Large brandy, Michael. Much appreciated.

FIRST MAN. I won't ask you again. What d' y' all want?

We see Ronny Renaldo walk across to the bar and sit, still singing and whistling.

RONNY RENALDO. If I were a blackbird I would whistle and sing.

FIRST MAN. He wants brain surgery.

But the second man hugs Ronny.

SECOND MAN. It was a lousy job anyway. *(He goes back to the bar as the glass-collector arrives.)*

COLLECTOR. Hurry along now ladies . . .

FIRST MAN. *(To Gnasher.)* What do you want, eh?

GNASHER. *(Between gnashes.)* Whisky and dry ginger please.

FIRST MAN. *(Gnashing back.)* It's my pleasure. *(He mimics him.)* Whisky and dry ginger please.

The barmaids are busy serving.

CHRISSIE. I'm goin' now. You have mine.

LOGGO. Hang on, I'll just . . .

The glass-collector takes Loggo's pint out of his hand.

LOGGO. . . . come with you.

Ronny Renaldo is at the bar whistling, surrounded by drinkers. We see the whole pub, noisy and chaotic. We hear the first man, 'Four more pints over here Joey for the playschool outing'. Ronny is still whistling.

FIRST MAN. Shut up Ronny, will y', y' getting on me tits.

The manager puts his head in his hands.

FIRST MAN. Where's my bevvy, then eh?

He grabs Loggo's arm as he and Chrissie go by.

Hey Loggo, you're not off are y'?

LOGGO. I've got to get out of this friggin' asylum.

FIRST MAN. Have another one. Two more pints.

The glass-collector takes his pint. He turns back.

Hey, where's my soddin' drink then? Hey, come back here.

Camera pans with Chrissie and Loggo. And then Yosser walks into the bar, looking dangerous and vacant. Chrissie and Loggo see Yosser.

LOGGO. Oh frig!

Yosser stands in the middle of the bar. Shake-hands walks up to him.

SHAKE-HANDS. Shake hands.

They are left alone together. The manager looks on horrified. Yosser stares at Shake-hands, and then down at Shake-hands' hands.

SHAKE-HANDS. Shake hands. Shake hands.

Shake-hands takes hold of Yosser's hand with both his hands and begins shaking it. Hardly any movement, not big at all. Yosser seems to stare curiously at Shake-hands. Then looks down at the hands gripping him, then back at Shake-hands' face. And as they stand close together staring at each other, Yosser butts him. Shake-hands reacts with a grin as his nose bursts, then goes to fall back and down. However, as he still has hold of Yosser's hand with both of his hands, he stays at sixty degrees for a second or so.

RONNY RENALDO. If I were a blackbird I would whistle and sing.

Then Yosser releases his grip. Shake-hands falls flat on his back. Yosser looks at him.

SHAKE-HANDS Another pint of bitter, boss. *(And out.)*

The pub crowd laugh. Yosser looks around and shrugs almost in apology and regret.

32. Exterior. The pub. Day.

*Chrissie and Loggo leave the pub. But still we can hear Ronny Renaldo
whistling. Loggo lights a cigarette. Chrissie joins him and they lean
against the wall.*

CHRISSIE. George is dead.

LOGGO. So y've said.

CHRISSIE. Yeah. But George is dead.

LOGGO. I know, Chrissie, *I know.*

CHRISSIE. But . . . you know what he stood for, don't y'?

LOGGO. What do you mean?

Chrissie shakes his head.

CHRISSIE. Yeah. Well that's dead an' all isn't it?

*As Chrissie finishes speaking and they begin to walk away, we hear a
chorus echoing from the pub. 'For Christ's sake, Ronny, I told you to
shut up. Alright Ronny you're gonna go.' Chrissie and Loggo stop and
listen.*

CHOIR. A one . . . a two . . . a three!

*And flying through the pub window comes Ronny Renaldo, still
holding on to his chair, and then landing on the pavement while still
sitting on his chair, unscathed. He sits facing the roadway. He begins
singing, cheerfully.*

RONNY RENALDO. 'Well I never felt more like singing the blues,
but I never thought I'd ever lose your love, dear, you got me
singin' the blues . . . I never felt more like cryin' all night.' etc

*We see the pub manager walking out of the same exit. He is putting
his coat on, as he goes. But he still has the large glass of whisky. He
approaches Chrissie and Loggo:*

PUB MANAGER. It's either them or me – and it's them.

*The manager goes out of our vision, across the road. Blindly we hear
a sharp squeal of brakes and the sound of a glass smashing, and a
car driver shouting abuse. Hey, you dick-head! Are you blind?*

The Manager stumbles on to the opposite side of the road and walks away.

CHRISSIE. There isn't a soul in there who is certified. They are all sane people.

There is a pause.

What is going wrong, Loggo? What is going wrong?

LOGGO. Everything, lah, everything.

They stay there as Yosser comes out of the entrance they came out of. He approaches them, but stays a few yards away. He glares out in the manner that they are staring out. They glance at him and look away. Chrissie glances up at the sky.

CHRISSIE. Beam me up, Scotty. Beam me up.

Loggo looks up too. Yosser looks at them, then looks up. We see their point of view – a derelict, part-demolished warehouse, 'Tate & Lyle's 1922', written across the front. Yosser turns to them and stares closely at them, then up again, then to them.

YOSSER. . . . Gizza job, go on, gizza job.

Chrissie and Loggo look at each other and visibly slump their shoulders. They turn and walk away, leaving Yosser. We see the warehouse being demolished, then we see the three of them walking along, Yosser following a few yards behind them, shambling along. He digs in a dustbin and finds a plastic bag, we finally see them walking along the road and into the sunset.

Freeze frame.

Boys From the Blackstuff

Five plays for television by
ALAN BLEASDALE
First broadcast by BBC Television September–October
1982

Director Philip Saville
Producer Michael Wearing
Music by Ilona Sekazc
Stunt Arranger Bill Weston
Fight Arranger Gareth Milne
Script Editor Roger Gregory
Production Associate Carol Parks
Production Managers
David Attwood
Andrew Smith
Bill Hartley
Production Assistants
Diane Coxon
Francine Brown
Sally Daniel
Assistant Floor Managers
Paul Braithwaite
Liddy Bennett
Designer Ian Ashurst
Design Assistant John Plush
Costume Designer Al Barnett
Costume Assistant Colin Bailey
Dressers
George Collins

Rachel Selby
Make Up Artist Maggie Thomas
Make Up Assistant Linda Webster
Graphics Designer Lesley Hope-Stone
Property Buyer Mike Preece
Lighting Dick Bentley
Planning
Steve Searley
Derek Price
Sound Supervisor Ramon Bailey
Sound Assistants
Tony Wass
Andy Redfern
Roger Waldron
Sound Recordist Alex Christison
Senior Cameraman Keith Salmon
Film Cameraman John Kenway
Second Cameramen
Brian Cave
Paul Woolston
Camera Assistant Keith Froggatt
Operator Ian Churchill
Gaffer Sparks Roy Carn
Grips Mike Patton
Videotape Editor Mike Bloore
Film Editor Greg Miller
Contracts Assistant Jonathan Macleish
Contracts Executive Manchester Chris Souter

The photographs used to illustrate this edition are copyright © BBC (*Moonlighters, Shop Thy Neighbour, George's Last Ride*), ©Express Newspapers (*Jobs for the Boys*) and © Liverpool Echo (*Yosser's Story*).

THE WORLD'S GREATEST NOVELISTS NOW AVAILABLE IN GRANADA PAPERBACKS

Simon Raven
Alms for Oblivion series

Fielding Gray	95p	☐
Sound the Retreat	95p	☐
The Sabre Squadron	95p	☐
The Rich Pay Late	95p	☐
Friends in Low Places	£1.25	☐
The Judas Boy	95p	☐
Places Where They Sing	95p	☐
Come Like Shadows	95p	☐
Bring Forth the Body	95p	☐
The Survivors	95p	☐

Other Titles

The Roses of Picardie	£1.50	☐
The Feathers of Death	35p	☐
Doctors Wear Scarlet	30p	☐

Paul Scott
The Raj Quartet

The Jewel in the Crown	£1.95	☐
The Day of the Scorpion	£1.95	☐
The Towers of Silence	£1.95	☐
A Division of the Spoils	£1.95	☐

Other Titles

The Bender	£1.95	☐
The Corrida at San Feliu	£1.25	☐
A Male Child	£1.50	☐
The Alien Sky	£1.25	☐
The Chinese Love Pavilion	£1.25	☐
The Mark of the Warrior	£1.95	☐
Johnnie Sahib	£1.25	☐
The Birds of Paradise	£1.50	☐
Staying On	£1.50	☐

THE WORLD'S GREATEST NOVELISTS NOW AVAILABLE IN GRANADA PAPERBACKS

Kurt Vonnegut

Breakfast of Champions	£1.95	☐
Mother Night	£1.95	☐
Slaughterhouse 5	£1.50	☐
Player Piano	£1.95	☐
Welcome to the Monkey House	£1.95	☐
God Bless You, Mr Rosewater	£1.25	☐
Happy Birthday, Wanda June	£1.50	☐
Slapstick	£1.25	☐
Wampeters, Foma & Granfalloons (non-fiction)	£1.95	☐
Between Time and Timbuktu (illustrated)	£1.50	☐
Jailbird	£1.95	☐
Palm Sunday	£1.95	☐

John Fowles

The Ebony Tower	£1.95	☐
The Collector	£1.95	☐
The French Lieutenant's Woman	£1.95	☐
The Magus	£2.50	☐
Daniel Martin	£2.50	☐
The Aristos (non-fiction)	£1.95	☐

Brian Moore

The Lonely Passion of Judith Hearne	£1.50	☐
I am Mary Dunne	£1.50	☐

GF481

**THE WORLD'S GREATEST NOVELISTS NOW AVAILABLE IN
GRANADA PAPERBACKS**

Angus Wilson

Such Darling Dodos	£1.50	☐
Latecall	£1.95	☐
The Wrong Set	£1.95	☐
For Whom the Cloche Tolls	£1.25	☐
A Bit Off the Map	£1.50	☐
As If By Magic	£2.50	☐
The Strange Ride of Rudyard Kipling (non-fiction)	£1.95	☐
Hemlock and After	£1.50	☐
No Laughing Matter	£1.95	☐
The Old Men at the Zoo	£1.95	☐
The Middle Age of Mrs Eliot	£1.95	☐
Setting the World on Fire	£1.95	☐

J B Priestley

Angel Pavement	£2.50	☐
Saturn Over The Water	£1.95	☐
Lost Empires	£1.95	☐
It's an Old Country	£1.95	☐
The Shapes of Sleep	£1.75	☐
The Good Companions	£2.50	☐

GF581

THE WORLD'S GREATEST NOVELISTS NOW AVAILABLE IN GRANADA PAPERBACKS

Gore Vidal
The American Trilogy

Washington DC	£1.95	☐
Burr	£1.95	☐
1876	£1.00	☐

Other Titles

A Thirsty Evil	£1.25	☐
The Judgment of Paris	£1.50	☐
The City and the Pillar	£1.25	☐
Julian	95p	☐
Two Sisters	£1.25	☐
Myron	£1.95	☐
Myra Breckinridge	£1.25	☐
Messiah	£1.25	☐
Williwaw	£1.95	☐
Kalki	£1.25	☐
A Search for the King	£1.25	☐
Dark Green, Bright Red	£1.25	☐
In A Yellow Wood	£1.25	☐
Matters of Fact and of Fiction	£1.50	☐
On Our Own Now (Collected Essays 1952-1972)	£1.50	☐
Creation	£1.95	☐

THE WORLD'S GREATEST NOVELISTS NOW AVAILABLE IN GRANADA PAPERBACKS

John O'Hara
Ourselves to Know	£1.50	☐
Ten North Frederick	£1.50	☐
A Rage to Live	£1.50	☐
From the Terrace	£2.50	☐
Butterfield 8	95p	☐
Appointment in Samarra	£1.95	☐

Norman Mailer
The Fight (non-fiction)	£1.25	☐
Cannibals and Christians (non-fiction)	£1.50	☐
The Presidential Papers	£1.50	☐
Advertisements for Myself	£1.95	☐
An American Dream	£1.95	☐
The Naked and The Dead	£2.50	☐
The Deer Park	£1.75	☐

Kingsley Amis
Ending Up	£1.25	☐
I Like It Here	£1.50	☐
That Uncertain Feeling	50p	☐
Girl 20	40p	☐
I Want It Now	60p	☐
The Green Man	95p	☐

GF881

All these books are available at your local bookshop or newsagent, and can be ordered direct from the publisher.

To order direct from the publisher just tick the titles you want and fill in the form below:

Name _____

Address _____

_____

Send to:
Granada Cash Sales
PO Box 11, Falmouth, Cornwall TR10 9EN

Please enclose remittance to the value of the cover price plus:

UK 45p for the first book, 20p for the second book plus 14p per copy for each additional book ordered to a maximum charge of £1.63.

BFPO and Eire 45p for the first book, 20p for the second book plus 14p per copy for the next 7 books, thereafter 8p per book.

Overseas 75p for the first book and 21p for each additional book.
